ELLIS ISLAND

ELLIS ISLAND

GATEWAY TO THE AMERICAN DREAM

PAMELA REEVES

CRESCENT BOOKS
New York

A FRIEDMAN GROUP BOOK

This 1991 edition published by Crescent Books,
distributed by Outlet Book Company, Inc.,
a Random House Company
225 Park Avenue South
New York, New York 10003

ISBN 0-517-05905-3

ELLIS ISLAND
Gateway to the American Dream
was prepared and produced by
Michael Friedman Publishing Group, Inc.
15 West 26th Street
New York, New York 10010

Editor: Sharyn Rosart
Designer: Susan Livingston
Photography Editor: Christopher Bain

Typeset by The Interface Group
Color separation by United South Sea Graphic Art
Printed and bound in Hong Kong by Leefung-Asco Printers Ltd.

8 7 6 5 4 3 2 1

ACKNOWLEDGMENTS

The author would like to thank

The Statue of Liberty/Ellis Island Foundation.

The publisher would like to thank

Brian Feeney and Diana Pardue of the National Park Service

for their assistance.

New York Public Library

TABLE OF

© Christopher C. Bain

CONTENTS

Lewis W. Hine/New York Public Library

© Christopher C. Bain

The Statue of Liberty has kept watch over New York Harbor for more than one hundred years, an enduring symbol of freedom and hope that welcomed immigrants to their new land.

INTRODUCTION

FPG International

Four out of ten Americans can trace their heritage via Ellis Island. Like the Statue of Liberty, it has been a powerfully evocative symbol to generations of immigrants.

Ellis Island opened in 1892 in the midst of an industrialization in the United States that drew eager workers from dozens of foreign nations; at its height in 1907, more than one million people came through its doors. Its decline began shortly after World War I, when Congress imposed severe restrictions on immigration, reflecting the attitudes of a society grown wary of foreigners. After 1924, immigration slowed to a trickle and Ellis Island fell into disuse. It was closed in 1954.

Courtesy National Park Service/Ellis Island Collection

Throughout its active years, Ellis Island showcased some of the best aspects of the United States, but also some of the worst. Its very existence was testimony to a class system—immigrants who could afford a first- or second-class ticket aboard the big ocean liners from Europe were briefly inspected aboard ship and allowed, in most cases, to pass directly into the United States. Only the poor were required to undergo an inspection at Ellis Island, and the poor comprised, by far, the majority of immigrants.

FPG International

OPPOSITE: *Clutching their belongings and identification tags, these immigrants disembark from the ferry that brought them from their ship and head toward the Main Building, where they would be processed.*

The Hebrew Immigrant Aid Society built this hut on Ellis Island for the benefit of immigrants who were detained on the island through the holiday of Succoth.

These steerage passengers—so-called because they traveled in the lowest levels of the ship, near the steering mechanisms—did not always receive a warm, or even humane, welcome. Treatment of the immigrants on Ellis Island varied over the years from tolerant to scandalous, and even the most honest and well-meaning administrators had trouble getting rid of the men of prey who tried to cheat the newcomers out of their few possessions or their often meager life savings. Indeed, the immigrants were easy marks, having just completed an uncomfortable or even wretched journey across the ocean, stepping onto shore in a country where they knew neither the language nor the money exchange-rates.

But if Ellis Island was a magnet for the unscrupulous, it also drew legions of kind-hearted missionaries and ethnic-aid societies, whose members guided their countrymen through the entry process, past the lurking pitfalls, and safely into the new land. The volunteers helped immigrants locate friends and get jobs.

It may be difficult for those living comfortably in America today to comprehend the forces that drove so many people to undertake a journey of such magnitude. But the immigrants—"your tired, your poor, your huddled masses"—had in common a hardy spirit.

Some were forced to leave their homes because of war, famine, or political or religious persecution. Some left unhappy family situations and struck out on their own. Most were drawn by the promise of a better life, and a country where plentiful and hard work led to prosperity.

Immigrants who came early to the United States often returned home for visits to describe for friends and relatives the opportunities that awaited the ambitious in the new land.

Others, accustomed to second-class status in their homeland, were impressed by the spirit of equality they found. Irishman James Richey, who immigrated in the early 1800s, related his first experience looking for work: "I went up to [a prospective employer] with my hat in my hand, as humble as any Irishman, and asked him if he wanted a person of my description. 'Put on yr hat,' said he, 'we are all a free people here, we all enjoy freedom and privileges.' He hesitated a little and said, 'I believe I do [want to hire you]'…and we closed our bargain."

*This stonework face (**ABOVE**) graced the facade of the French Renaissance-style Main Building (**OPPOSITE**) that was erected in 1900 after fire destroyed the earlier wooden buildings. Its rich architecture was an impressive sight to many of the immigrants as they arrived at Ellis Island.*

Today, to mark the centennial—1892-1992—the federal government has restored Ellis Island as a historical museum.

This book is the story of Ellis Island and those it welcomed. It is a celebration of the country that embraced the newcomers and a tribute to those who took up the challenge of a new life in America.

National Park Service/photo: Brian Feeney

A 1911 view of the buildings at the Battery, including Castle Garden, which was built in 1807 in preparation for the War of 1812.

CASTLE GARDEN

CHAPTER ONE

New York Public Library

When Ellis Island opened in 1892, it marked the passage of immigration from state to federal control, a change sought by Washington for two reasons: to appease the voices in society that were raising objections to the continuing unregulated flow of newcomers; and to deal with the corruption and cronyism that mired down the entire process, especially in New York, where most of the immigrants landed.

Between 1880 and 1900, nine million immigrants entered the country, the largest number of new arrivals in any twenty-year period. This alarmed many Americans, in part because of a shift in the nationality of the immigrants. The earliest settlers in the United States were from northern and western Europe, primarily England, Ireland, Germany, and the Scandinavian countries. Those nations continued to provide the bulk of immigrants until the late 1800s, when people from southern and eastern Europe began to predominate. By 1896, Italy, Russia, Poland, Spain, Greece, Eastern Europe, and Austria-Hungary were the sources of the majority of immigrants, and they continued to be until 1924, when a stiff immigration-restriction law was imposed.

America was undergoing a major transformation from a rural to an urban society during this period that led to unprecedented prosperity, despite several depressions. In

OPPOSITE: A scene depicting the infamous Chicago riot of 1886 shows a dynamite bomb exploding among the police.

This old manual typewriter was found among the debris during the restoration.

© Brian Feeney

1880, the census found that only 28 percent of the people lived in urban communities; by 1900 the urban figure had risen to 40 percent. The change was accompanied by a huge growth in the iron, steel, mining, and lumber industries and such major developments as the telephone, the automobile, linotype, electric light, the phonograph, and the cash register. These industries and their offshoots required millions of laborers and provided the economic draw for those in less prosperous European nations.

Despite some early mutual distrust, many of the immigrants joined the newly developed American labor unions, eventually becoming a major force in the movement. Their struggle for such rights as the eight-hour work day led to bloody strikes and

violent confrontations. In 1886 alone, there were nearly 1,600 strikes involving 600,000 workers, one of them culminating in Chicago's infamous Haymarket Riot, in which eight policemen were killed and more than sixty people wounded.

FPG International

Many Americans blamed the unions and their immigrant members for the Haymarket deaths, and prejudice against foreigners increased. With federal control of immigration, it was felt, it would be much easier to enforce restrictions that the states were unable or unwilling to impose.

At the same time, in the late 1880s, there was a public outcry against the abuses at New York City's Castle Garden, which had opened in 1855 as the nation's first receiving-station for immigrants. During its thirty-five years of operation, Castle Garden handled nine million immigrants, among them Samuel Gompers (1863), first president of the AFL-CIO, and Jacob Riis (1870), journalist and social reformer.

Castle Garden, at the southern tip of Manhattan, was built by the federal government in 1807 in preparation for the 1812 war with England. After the war, the fort was named Castle Clinton in honor of Governor DeWitt Clinton of New York. It was ceded to New York City in the 1820s and later leased to a private firm as an amusement park. By 1839, it had become a fashionable concert hall. Jenny Lind, the Swedish opera singer, made her American debut there in 1850, and her outstanding performance spread the name Castle Garden throughout the country.

Castle Garden –
Built by Fed-Gov
en 1807 for 1812
war with England

en declined, however, so did the concert

make an ideal place to receive immigrants,

embark directly into the city after passing

seases were found aboard

temmed in part from the

hey landed, and also from

. New York, as America's

he most immigrants of any

ms.

d been touring the United

ut he visited the steerage

American Notes, he con-

assengers with the experi-

at 3, and took our tea at half-past seven. We had abundance of amusements and dinner was not the least among them…then we had chess for those who played it, whist, cribbage, books, backgammon and shovelboard. In all weathers, fair or foul, calm or windy, we were every one on deck, walking up and down in pairs, lying in the boats, leaning over the side or chatting in a lazy group together. We had no lack of music…."

The boat carried about a hundred passengers in steerage, "a little world of poverty" that included people denied entry into America and those who had failed to make a living in their new land.

Some of them had been in America but three days, some but three months, and some had gone out in the last voyage of that very ship in which they were now returning home. Others had sold their clothes to raise the passage-money, and had hardly rags to cover them; others had no food and lived upon the charity of the rest; and one man, it was

Samuel Gompers, cigar-maker and eventual founder of the American Federation of Labor, emigrated to America with his parents from Britain in 1863.

FPG International

discovered nearly at the end of the voyage, not before—for he kept his secret close and did not court compassions—had had no sustenance whatever but the bones and scraps of fat he took from the plates used in the after-cabin dinner, when they were put out to be washed.[1]

Steerage passengers were denied the elegant dinners and luxurious quarters enjoyed by first- and second-class voyagers.

Dickens demanded an end to the abusive system that allowed shipowners to sell space to unscrupulous men, who then sought out as many poor immigrants as possible to fill it, thereby making a handsome profit while ensuring terrible traveling conditions for the passengers. But with so much money to be made and little government regulation, improvements were slow to come.

In 1845, just three years after Dickens' journey, Ireland was hit with a famine stemming from crop failures of the main peasant food—potatoes. Over the next decade, 1.5 million Irish citizens set out for the United States. The very poorest took the cheaper route to Canada—then called British North America—and many of them were near starvation when they boarded. Immigrants at the time were required to provide their own food for the journey, and it was not uncommon for them to run out of provisions if the ship ran into storms and was at sea for two or three months. Lack of food, poor ventilation in the jam-packed steerage quarters, and contagious diseases took a fearsome toll.

In 1847, the year in which more than 214,000 Irish set out for North America "running away from fever and disease and hunger with money scarcely sufficient to pay passage for and find food for the voyage,"[2] 30 percent of those bound for British North America died. The death toll among those sailing for the United States was 9 percent.

News of the deaths shocked both America and Britain and resulted in new laws passed over the next eight years requiring shipowners or their agents to provide food for immigrants during the journey. The ocean liners also were required to have at least two ventilators in steerage and covered hatchways that could be left open even during a storm. New York inspected the ships and imposed penalties for breaking the law, but the fines were not high enough to deter greedy shipowners. Death rates on the ships remained high.

In the words of Charles Dickens, the steerage passengers' quarters below-deck were an appalling "little world of poverty."

At about the same time these new laws were passed, New York decided to turn Castle Garden into a receiving station for the immigrants to protect them from the gaggle of swindlers who accosted them with offers of housing, food, trinkets, and railway tickets as they stepped off the boat.

Irish immigrants who boarded the ocean liners at Liverpool, in England, often fell victim to the network of crooked shippers, innkeepers, ticket agents, porters, and money changers who infested the docks. If the immigrant survived those swindlers, he

New York Public Library

too frequently met up with the same type of lowlifes when he reached New York. "People may think that if they get safe through Liverpool they are all right," said one immigrant, "but I can assure you that there is greater robberies done in New York on immigrants than there is in Liverpool."[3]

Wrote another immigrant, "I have met with so much deception since we have landed on the shores of the New World that I am fearful of trusting anyone."[4]

To provide the immigrants with a better start, New York officials fenced off Castle Garden, in order to maintain control over those who entered and left the receiving house.

This system improved the immigrant's prospects for a time, and Castle Garden was able to function smoothly due to a drop in the number of newcomers during the years around the Civil War. In 1871, *Harper's New Monthly Magazine* described the procedure for new arrivals:

Steerage Accommodation Unequalled for Ventilation, Light, and Care for Passengers' Comfort.

Passengers cannot do better than take their Tickets from our Agents before leaving home.

WHITE STAR LINE

UNITED STATES   MAIL STEAMERS.

BRITANNIC.   CELTIC.   GERMANIC.   ADRIATIC.   BALTIC.
REPUBLIC.   OCEANIC.   GAELIC.   BELGIC.

THESE WELL-KNOWN, FAST MAIL STEAMERS SAIL FROM

LIVERPOOL TO NEW YORK,

EVERY THURSDAY,

GERMANIC,	Thursday, Aug. 31	BRITANNIC,	Thursday, Oct. 26
CELTIC,	,, Sept. 7	GERMANIC,	,, Nov. 9
BRITANNIC,	,, 21	CELTIC,	,, ,, 16
GERMANIC,	,, Oct. 5	BRITANNIC,	,, ,, 30
CELTIC,	,, 12		

Calling at QUEENSTOWN on the Following Day.

These splendid, full-powered, First-class Iron Screw Steamers are among the largest and most powerful vessels afloat, and are distinguished for the shortness and regularity of their passages, and the completeness and comfort of their passenger accommodation.

SALOON PASSAGE, 15, 18, AND 21 GUINEAS EACH BERTH,

According to State Room selected, all having equal Privileges in Saloon. Children under Twelve Years, Half-Fare. Infants Free.

Return Tickets, available for one year, issued at Reduced Rates.

These rates include a Liberal Table and Steward's Fee, without Wines or Liquors, which can be obtained on board. £5 Deposit is required to secure Cabin Berths, the balance to be paid the day before sailing. Luggage will go on board with the Passengers in the Tender that leaves the Landing Stage for the Steamer on the day of sailing.

STEERAGE FARE to NEW YORK, BOSTON, or PHILADELPHIA,

Six Guineas (£6 6s.) including a plentiful supply of cooked Provisions.

Children under Eight years Half Fare, and Infants under 12 months £1 1s.

The Steerage accommodation in these Steamers is of the very highest character, the rooms are unusually spacious, well lighted, ventilated, and warmed, and passengers of this class will find their comfort carefully studied.

Passengers will be provided with Berths to sleep in, each adult having a separate berth; but they have to provide themselves with a Plate Mug, Knife, Fork, Spoon, and Water Can, also Bedding,—all of which can be purchased on shore for about 10/-. MARRIED COUPLES, WITH THEIR CHILDREN, WILL BE BERTHED TOGETHER. FEMALES will be Berthed in rooms by themselves.

BILL OF FARE.—Each Passenger will be supplied with 3 quarts of Water daily, and with as much Provisions as he can eat, which are all of the best quality, and which are examined and put on board under the inspection of Her Majesty's Emigration Officers, *and cooked and served out by the Company's servants*.

BREAKFAST AT EIGHT O'CLOCK.—Coffee, Sugar, and fresh Bread and Butter, or Biscuit and Butter, or Oatmeal Porridge and Molasses.

DINNER AT ONE O'CLOCK.—Soup and Beef, Pork, or Fish, according to the day of the week, with Bread and Potatoes, and on Sunday Pudding will be added.

SUPPER AT SIX O'CLOCK.—Tea, Sugar, Biscuit, and Butter. Oatmeal Gruel will be supplied at 8 p.m. when necessary.

LUGGAGE.—TEN CUBIC FEET will be allowed for each adult Steerage Passenger, free; for all over that quantity a charge of 1s. 6d. for each cubic foot will be made. Steerage Passengers must have their luggage ready to go on board the Steamer on the morning of the day of sailing.

Passengers are landed at the Government Depôt, Castle Garden, New York, where they can purchase Tickets for, and receive every information respecting the departure of Trains, Steam-boats, &c.

These Steamers run in connection with the Erie Railway from New York—the shortest and best route to the West, North and South-Western States; and Passengers are Booked through at low rates, to all parts of the States, Canada, Aspinwall and San Francisco, also to Australia, New Zealand, China and Japan, by the Pacific Railway and Mail Steam-ship Company.

All passengers are liable to be rejected, who, upon examination, are found to be lunatic idiot, deaf, dumb, blind, maimed, or infirm, or above the age of 60 years; or widow with a child or children, or any woman without a husband with a child or children; or any person unable to take care of himself (or herself) without becoming a public charge, or who from any attending circumstances are likely to become a public charge, or who from sickness or disease, existing at the time of departure, are likely soon to become a public charge. Sick persons or widows with children cannot be taken, nor lame persons, unless full security be given for the Bonds to be entered into by the State Government, that the parties will not become chargeable to the State.

ALL STEERAGE PASSENGERS embarking at Liverpool must be at the Office of the Agents, 10, Water Street, Liverpool, not later than 6 p.m. of the day before the advertised date of sailing, when the balance of the passage-money must be paid, or the deposit forfeited.

All Steerage Passengers embarking at Queenstown must be at the Office of the Agent at Queenstown (Cork) not later than Six o'clock p.m. of the day before sailing when the balance of the passage money must be paid, or the deposit forfeited, and all Passengers will have strictly to conform to the Rules laid down by the Company. In order to meet the requirements of the Government Emigration Officer, Contract Tickets will be issued for the Noon of the day previous to the advertised date of sailing.

AN EXPERIENCED SURGEON IS CARRIED BY EACH STEAMER.

STEWARDESSES IN STEERAGE TO ATTEND THE WOMEN AND CHILDREN. NO FEES OR EXTRA CHARGES

Passage can be engaged and Tickets obtained from any Agent of the "White Star" Line, or by sending name, age, and occupation, together with a deposit of One Pound on each berth, to

Wells & Holohan, Railway Agents, 6 Eden-quay, and 9

North Wall, Dublin

"Slowly, one by one the newcomers passed the two officers, whose study it is to register every immigrant's name, birthplace and destination in large folios....On they passed, one by one, in single file till a few steps farther down they came to the desk of the so-called booker, a clerk of the Railway Association, whose duty it is to ascertain the destination of each passenger, and furnish him with a printed slip, upon which this is set forth, with the number of tickets wanted, and their cost in currency."[5]

Harper's said this system was a great improvement, since the immigrant paid a fair price for the railroad ticket. The magazine noted that those who bought their tickets outside Castle Garden had often been swindled.

The article also noted that immigrants could exchange their money inside Castle Garden, where the fair trading-rates were posted daily.

The Central Railroad of New Jersey Terminal took immigrants to points west. About one-third of newcomers stayed in New York City.

Outside Castle Garden, however, the rule was still "traveler beware," as a case recited by Robert Louis Stevenson attested. In "The Amateur Emigrant," he described two young men—M'Naughten and a friend—who landed in New York, traveled to Boston, spent the day carousing, and set out at midnight to find an inn. They settled on a cheap hotel: The room had a bed, a chair, and a couple of framed pictures, "one close above the head of the bed, and the other opposite the foot, and both curtained."

Curtained portraits were in fashion at the time, especially for "works of art more than usually skittish in the subject."

Perhaps anticipating such a picture, M'Naughten's companion pulled back one of the curtains and "was startlingly disappointed." The curtains covered not a portrait but a hole in the wall that would allow anyone outside the room to reach through and take a purse from the sleeping traveler—or even strangle him.

> *M'Naughten and his comrade stared at each other like Vasco's seamen, 'with a wild surmise' and then the latter, catching up the lamp, ran to the other frame and roughly raised the curtain. There he stood, petrified; and M'Naughten, who had followed, grasped him by the wrist in terror. They could see into another room, larger in size than that which they occupied, where three men sat crouching and silent in the dark. For a second or so these five persons looked each other in the eyes, then the curtain was dropped and M'Naughten and his friend made but one bolt of it out of the room and downstairs.... They gave up all notion of a bed and walked the streets of Boston till the morning.[6]*

Despite all the perils of travel, immigration by the 1880s was again on the rise, and attitudes toward the newcomers were becoming increasingly negative. There had been race riots in San Francisco against the Chinese, who comprised seventeen percent of the population and worked for low wages for railroad builders. Feelings ran so strong that in 1882 Congress banned Chinese immigrants from entering the United States. Another law, passed that same year, excluded "any convict, lunatic, idiot or any person unable to take care of himself or herself without becoming a public charge." Three years later, in 1885, labor unions succeeded in getting a law passed to stop businessmen from importing men willing to work for little money, which undercut the wage minimums the unions had finally been able to win. This Alien Contract Labor Law was administered by federal agents, working side by side with state authorities at Castle Garden.

In this atmosphere, concern for the welfare of the immigrant declined and so did the state of the bureaucracy at Castle Garden. New York newspapers, led by Joseph Pulitzer's *The World*, charged that the swindlers who had long lurked outside the

A traditional Chinese drugstore run by immigrants. A popular store might fill up to 100 prescriptions a day for immigrants eager to find remedies from home.

receiving station had now insinuated themselves inside and that cheating, misleading, and stealing were running rampant. In 1887, in an article titled "Cogent Reasons for the Abolition of the Emigration Commission," *The World* complained especially about the contract on rail transportation for immigrants leaving New York that Castle Garden had awarded to a few lines:

> It [Castle Garden] was organized in order that the hundreds of thousands of immigrants that come to these shores every year might be protected and cared for until they reached their destination; but instead of doing this, the commission throws the immigrants into the hands of a heartless railroad pool that treats them most shamefully and squeezes all it can out of them.... The immigrants are not only huddled like cattle in the uncomfortable and foul-smelling cars of this unlawful pool, that run on a freight schedule, taking two days instead of one to reach Chicago, but they are deprived of the right to select by which one even of the pool lines they shall purchase their tickets, and are charged exorbitant rates for baggage.[7]

The World also cited a number of cases of immigrants being detained for no good reason and mistreated in the process. Especially galling was the case of Ingjerd Jonson, a single woman with a child who had come to the United States to live with her sister and other family members.

Even though her relatives came forward and assured authorities that Jonson would not wind up as "an object for public charity," she was detained at Castle Garden for days. *The World* said she was forced to sleep on bare wooden benches, was given only bread and milk to eat, and complained that she had been "criminally assaulted by George Ivern, one of the employees of the Garden."[8]

The World demanded an investigation into the case, and Jonson eventually was turned over to her relatives.

Her case and others cited in newspapers led to several investigations and reports, culminating in 1890 with a decision by Washington to take immigration totally out of New York's hands and make it a federal charge. The stage was set for Ellis Island to make its debut—but not without a lot of controversy and delay.

An engraving of a typical day at Castle Garden in 1884 shows the immigrants huddled with their bundles and trunks as they wait to be processed.

A new generation of Americans. Many of the immigrants who came to America as children retain vivid memories of their experiences at Ellis Island.

THE GOLDEN DOORWAY INTO AMERICA OPENS

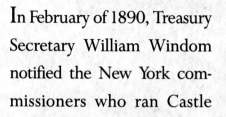

CHAPTER TWO

FPG International

In February of 1890, Treasury Secretary William Windom notified the New York commissioners who ran Castle Garden that the federal government would assume responsibility for immigration, starting that April. Windom came to his decision after several years of discussions and investigations. Two years earlier, Congressman Melbourne Ford of Michigan had done a study of Castle Garden and concluded it was hopelessly inadequate.

Ford reported that the committee had visited Castle Garden several times and found the facilities too small to handle the large number of immigrants arriving daily. As a result, he said, "Large numbers of persons not lawfully entitled to land in the United States are annually received at this port. In fact, one of the commissioners of immigration himself testified that the local administration of affairs at Castle Garden, by the method and system now followed, was a perfect farce."[1]

Windom decided that if the federal government was to succeed in controlling immigration and getting rid of the corruption that had grown up around the process, it must isolate the newcomers as soon as they arrived. He set his sights on building a federal immigration station in New York Harbor, and his first choice was Bedloe, or Liberty, Island, site of the Statue of Liberty.

This idea aroused immediate opposition, led by *The New York World:* "Mr. Windom has a theory that the erection of barracks on Liberty Island for the accommodation of 8,000 immigrants will embellish and beautify the island. The secretary has a fine eye for beauty. The purpose of locating the colossal Statue of Liberty on a little island in our

Governor's Island was originally set aside as part of the "Fort of New York" in 1698. At the turn of the century it held army barracks.

FPG International

harbor was to have it spring majestically from the very bosom of the water, as it were. To surround it with buildings will be to dwarf and humiliate it....Cannot something be done in Congress at once to prevent this outrage?"[2]

Another possibility was Governor's Island, but it was used at the time as a military base, and the army was quick to put forth vigorous objections to sharing its reservation with a flood of immigrants.

A congressional committee assigned to settle the question noted all the furor over Bedloe and Governor's islands and voted to take the path of least resistance. In April 1890, it decided the new immigration station would be built on Ellis Island, in upper New York Bay near the New Jersey shore.

Windom opposed the idea, since the island was only three acres (1.2 hectares) in size and set in water so shallow it was difficult to reach by boat. But by choosing Ellis Island,

An old sketch showing the U.S. Navy's powder magazines at Ellis Island, which were later converted to dormitories.

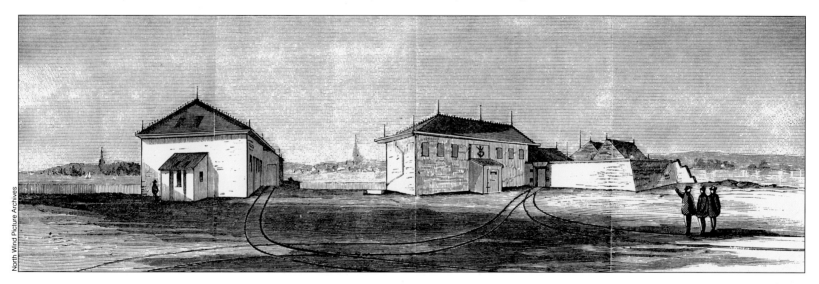

North Wind Picture Archives

Congress not only avoided offending powerful interests, it also solved another annoying problem. Ellis Island housed a number of naval munitions magazines, which led to periodic protests over the danger of housing such powerful explosives so close to the urban centers of New York and New Jersey. With the plans for a new immigration station, the explosives were removed from the island at once.

Over the next twenty months, Ellis Island was enlarged, the channel dredged, docks built, and a series of wooden buildings constructed—a large, two-story hall for registra-

tion and inspection, a hospital, a laundry, and a utility plant. The old navy magazines were converted to dormitories. The total cost was $500,000.

While the site for the new immigration station was being made ready, new arrivals were received at a makeshift federal office in a granite building near Castle Garden that had been constructed for the U.S. Customs Bureau. This building, known as the Barge Office, was staffed largely with holdovers from Castle Garden and was even more cramped and just as corrupt. So it was with some relief that the immigration officers moved into the new buildings at Ellis Island, which formally opened on New Year's Day, 1882. *The New York Times* described the event the next day:

> *There were three big steamships in the harbor waiting to land their passengers and there was much anxiety among the newcomers to be the first landed at the new station. The honor was reserved for a little rosy-cheeked Irish girl. She was Annie Moore, 15 years of age, lately a resident of County Cork and yesterday one of the 148 steerage passengers landed from the...steamship* Nevada....

ABOVE: *A contemporary newspaper illustration shows the construction of the new immigrant receiving station at Ellis Island.*

OPPOSITE: *This drawing of immigrants detained at Ellis Island shows the early wooden buildings that were originally erected there, and the "wire screened enclosure" where detainees were held.*

As soon as the gangplank was run ashore Annie tripped across it and hurried into the big building that almost covers the entire island. By a prearranged plan she was escorted to a registry desk which was temporarily occupied by Mr. Charles M. Henley, the former private secretary of Secretary Windom.... "When the little voyager had been registered, Col. Weber [the commissioner of immigration] presented her with a $10 gold piece and made a short address of congratulations and welcome. It was the first United States coin she had ever seen and the largest sum of money she had ever possessed...."

In the same article, *The Times* described how the 445,987 immigrants who would pass through Ellis Island that year were to be officially received. The wharves were large enough to receive immigrants from two ships simultaneously. Once ashore, they went straight into a giant hall and a maze of aisles where they waited their turn to talk with a registry clerk. Those who failed to pass the initial inspection were "placed in a wire-screened enclosure." The rest were separated into groups, depending on whether they planned to stay in New York or were taking a train to another destination. "There is an information bureau in the building for the benefit of those seeking friends or relatives among the immigrants. There are also telegraph and railroad ticket offices and a money exchanger's office."[3]

Ellis Island opened during a period when American opinion on immigration was divided. Strong forces advocated limiting the numbers and kinds of people allowed into the country, and while they did not succeed in ending the nation's "Open Door" policy until the 1920s, they did manage to impose increasingly severe restrictions.

One of the most far-reaching changes during this period was a decision to make steamship companies responsible for inspecting immigrants before bringing them to America and requiring them to pay return passage for any passengers rejected.

The ship owners had to prepare information sheets on each passenger—no more than thirty to a sheet—that could be cross-checked when the immigrants were examined at Ellis Island. The list had to include name, age, sex, marital status, occupation, nationality, last residence, destination, and whether the immigrant could read and write. It also asked: whether the immigrant had paid his own passage and had tickets through to his final destination; whether he was under contract to work in the United States; if he had ever been in prison, in a poorhouse, or suffered deformities or illnesses; and whether he was a polygamist.

With these new restrictions, those seeking to control immigration hoped to reduce the number of foreigners entering the United States each year. But it was not to be.

This view from the northeast shows the original Main Building and other wooden structures.

Courtesy National Park Service/Ellis Island Collection

*After the 1897 fire destroyed the old pine buildings at Ellis Island,
the handsome red brick and stone Main Building pictured here was
erected, to the relief of the immigration commissioner, who had
long feared a catastrophe.*

THE GREAT HALL FIRE AND THE ERA OF REFORM

CHAPTER THREE

New York Public Library

Fire broke out on Ellis Island shortly after midnight on June 14, 1897, just five years after it had opened. The buildings, made of pine, were completely destroyed, but the 140 immigrants held on the island at the time escaped unharmed, along with all the employees. The immigration commissioner, Joseph Senner, saw the destruction in a positive light: "Ever since I have been in office the fear of something like this fire has haunted me, and now that it has come and no lives were lost I am glad of it," he told the *New York Tribune.* "A row of unsightly, ramshackle tinderboxes has been removed, and when the government rebuilds, it will be forced to put up decent fireproof structures."[1]

Within a month rebuilding started, this time with fireproof materials. The main hall, 385 feet (116 m) long and 165 feet (50 m) wide, was brick over a steel frame. Separate buildings contained a restaurant, laundry, bathhouse, and hospital. The total cost was $1.5 million.

The new station, which opened on December 17, 1900, was well-received. *The New York Times* commented, "One has only to remember the old ramshackle structure to be able to appreciate the magnificent and admirably arranged new quarters. Situated on one of the most prominent locations in the harbor, the new station is an imposing as well as a pleasing addition to the picturesque waterfront of the metropolis."

The Times went on to describe how the station would function:

> *Every detail of the exacting and confusing service to which its uses are to be dedicated were considered in perfecting the interior plans....When the immigrant is landed from the barges he will pass through an imposing private entrance, made as nearly as possible free from the observation of the curious, besides protecting him during bad weather. He then goes to the second floor, the entire center of which is given up to the examining department, where he is inspected by the medical authorities, and the officials of other branches of the service who pass upon his eligibility to land....*
>
> *The railings forming the network of the aisles, in which the immigrants are placed in alphabetical order, according to nationality, give the great amphitheatre the appearance of an immense spider web....It is estimated that 5,000 persons can be thoroughly examined with perfect ease, and in an emergency 3,000 more by the application of a little added energy on the part of the examiners."[2]*

National Archives

ABOVE: *The completed Main Building, June 30, 1900. The station opened to receive its first immigrants on December 17 of the same year.*

OPPOSITE: *These workers are erecting the first stones of the new Main Building at Ellis Island, April 20, 1899.*

Unfortunately, the same kind words could not be said for the administration of the island. After the fire, operations were temporarily transferred back to the Barge Office and Senner left office. He was replaced by Thomas Fitchie, a politically active New York Republican who put one of his assistants, Edward McSweeney, in charge of operations. At the same time, a top labor leader, Terence Powderly, became commissioner of the Bureau of Immigration in Washington.

In his autobiography, Powderly recalled the problems he encountered: The new immigrants were overcharged for food and cheated in money exchanges. Their relatives were required to pay a fee to get into Ellis Island to greet them. Immigrants who planned to travel to other cities were given false information about the distances involved and overcharged for the tickets.

Powderly appointed a commission to gather evidence, and in June 1900, eleven Ellis Island employees were fired.[3]

OPPOSITE: *In the Registry Room, shown here before the installation of the vaulted Guastavino ceiling, immigrants sat on long wooden benches that replaced the original iron-piped alleys in 1911 until it was their turn to speak to an inspector.*

BELOW: *A group of immigrants puts ashore at Ellis Island, while a line of crowded ferry boats waits patiently to disgorge yet more passengers.*

New York Public Library

At times, corruption was rife at Ellis Island and detainees might "persuade" dishonest inspectors to accept them with a well-placed bribe.

OPPOSITE: *In the early days of the new station, immigrants attempting to change money were often cheated by unscrupulous concessionaires.*

Edward Steiner, a minister who traveled in steerage several times to see for himself what conditions were like, also found Ellis Island unsavory during this time:

> *I knew that the money changers were 'crooked,' so I passed a 20 mark piece to one of them for exchange, and was cheated out of nearly 75 percent of my money. My change was largely composed of new pennies, whose brightness was well calculated to deceive any newcomer.*
>
> *At another time I was approached by an inspector who, in a very friendly way, intimated that I might have difficulty in being permitted to land, and that money judiciously placed might accomplish something.*
>
> *A Bohemian girl whose acquaintance I had made on the steamer came to me with tears in her eyes and told me that one of the inspectors had promised to pass her quickly, if she would promise to meet him at a certain hotel. In heartbroken tones she asked: "Do I look like that?"*[4]

Newspapers at the time were full of stories about thievery at Ellis Island, and in the summer of 1901, it was discovered that immigration inspectors had been selling forged citizenship papers to immigrants, allowing them to bypass Ellis Island altogether.

When Theodore Roosevelt became president he took immediate steps to clean up the problems. In a letter dated October 1901, he wrote, "As for Fitchie, there is a consensus of testimony to his utter inefficiency," and "Every really good man whom I have met who knows anything about that office has agreed in believing McSweeney to be corrupt."[5]

Roosevelt replaced Powderly with another labor leader, Frank Sargent, and ousted both Fitchie and McSweeney. After a search, he found the man he thought could run Ellis Island well—William Williams, a wealthy Wall Street lawyer whom he did not know personally but who had a fine reputation and some government experience.

Williams became commissioner of Ellis Island on April 28, 1902, and served until 1905 and then again from 1909 to 1913. He moved swiftly and effectively to dislodge the powerful, entrenched forces at the receiving station. The first thing he did was to put employees on notice that if they continued to act like thugs and thieves, they would be out of a job. Williams posted a notice around the island announcing:

Immigrants must be treated with kindness and consideration. Any government official violating the terms of this notice will be recommended for dismissal from the service. Any other person so doing will be forthwith required to leave Ellis Island. It is earnestly requested that any violation hereof, or any instance of any kind of improper treatment of immigrants at Ellis Island, or before they leave the Barge Office, be promptly brought to the attention of the commissioner.[6]

A number of employees caught cheating immigrants were fired after this notice appeared, and soon the workforce, long accustomed to tolerance of petty thievery, realized that open-palm days were at an end.

Williams realized that if he was going to reform Ellis Island he would have to take on the politically powerful forces that ran the lucrative

North Wind Picture Archives

OPPOSITE: *An aerial view of Ellis Island, shot at night from a plane, shows the original island on the right, and Island 2, added in 1899, on the left.*

As Commissioner of Immigration, labor leader Terence Powderly tried to clean up some of the corruption at Ellis Island, appointing a committee which eventually fired eleven employees.

concessions on the island. Within months of taking office he terminated the contracts for the food, baggage, and money exchange concessions. New York Republicans howled, but Roosevelt stood by his commissioner and soon an immigrant arriving at Ellis Island could be fairly sure he would not be robbed or insulted while being processed.

Williams recorded these victories in his scrapbooks:

> *There was brisk bidding for the new contracts, the old concessionaires feeling confident that with their strong political influence and being in the saddle they would be chosen again. All had strong Republican backing.*
>
> *What I did was to make a clean sweep with resulting consternation. I had considered not only the amounts of the bids but the standing and character of the bidders. Many of the unsuccessful bidders through their political agents and personal friends made direct protest to the president...[and] the president deemed it of sufficient importance to grant all the bidders a hearing at the White House (a very unusual proceeding). I was present and roundly abused but emerged triumphant, for all my recommendations were approved by the president himself, and in doing so he turned down politicians and friends alike.*[7]

FPG International

Theodore Roosevelt surprised immigrants and employees alike by making an unannounced visit to Ellis Island in September of 1903, where he liberated a woman and her four children who had been detained for nearly two months.

OPPOSITE: *A Czechoslovakian family posed on the lawn at Ellis Island before boarding a train to Indiana, where they settled on a farm.*

While he succeeded in making Ellis Island much more honest and efficient than it had ever been, Williams made a lot of enemies, and not only among the politicians he humiliated. He sided philosophically with the forces that wanted to restrict immigration and he felt the eastern and southern European peoples coming into the United States in the early 1900s did not measure up to the English and Germans who had predominated in the earlier wave of immigration. He excluded large numbers of immigrants who would have had an easier time getting in under earlier administrators.

As a result, throughout his two terms as commissioner, Williams fought a running battle with ethnic groups and publications that favored a more lax policy, including the German-Americans who dominated the shipping lines transporting the immigrants. He was forced to spend much of his time answering charges and responding to investigations, including one initiated by Roosevelt.

New York Public Library

The president made a surprise visit to Ellis Island on September 16, 1903, probably in response to the angry complaints that were frequently printed in the nation's German-American newspapers. During the visit, Roosevelt "held an impromptu hearing in the case of a woman and her four children, who, bound about with official red tape, had been languishing in the detention pen for nearly two months and promptly set them free."[8]

Williams not only survived the investigation but drew compliments from a commission the president had appointed to look into conditions at Ellis Island. The commission said Williams was "entitled to the highest commendation for the indefatigable zeal and intelligent supervision he has exercised in administering the affairs of the Ellis Island station and for the humane consideration he has invariably shown to the immigrants while they remained under his jurisdiction."[9]

Williams and Roosevelt parted ways, however, in a confrontation over Roosevelt's refusal to fire a personal friend he had put in place as the second in command at Ellis

This photograph of the ferry disgorging its load of passengers shows the original cast iron and glass canopy that sheltered the immigrants as they walked to the Main Building.

Island. Williams, who sometimes worked almost around the clock at the immigration station, found the man incompetent and lazy. He resigned in anger over the matter in January 1905.

Roosevelt was sorry to see him go but the man he appointed to replace Williams, Robert Watchorn, kept the island running smoothly and honestly and was considered a more compassionate administrator. Watchorn served for four years, and when Roosevelt left office, President William Taft reappointed Williams to the post.

During the peak period of immigration in the early 1900s, Ellis Island was generally well run. Even so, it had continuous problems, as the millions of immigrants who came through it could attest.

Immigrants who were to travel to their final destinations by railroad had their railway tickets pinned to their lapels. Here, a German family is tagged by an official.

Lewis W. Hine/New York Public Library

After an ocean passage of long and uncomfortable weeks, several generations of immigrants anxiously await their chance to begin a new life in America.

ISLAND OF HOPE, ISLAND OF TEARS

CHAPTER FOUR

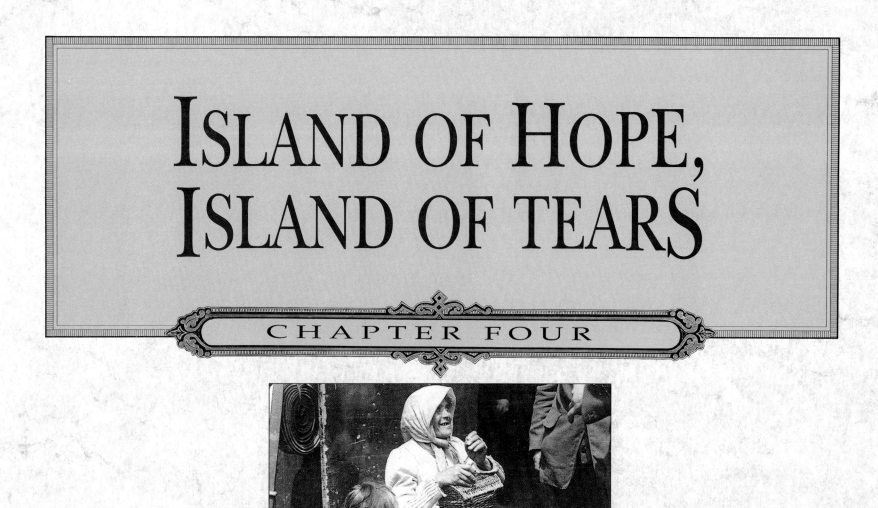

FPG International

The immigrants who passed through Ellis Island have left a fascinating history of their experiences in letters to relatives and in stories passed down through the generations.

It was a traumatic time for many, made worse by frightening tales told by those who had come before. As many as two percent of the newcomers were sent home again each year, without ever setting foot on American shores outside Ellis Island. One out of five immigrants had to spend long, anxious days or weeks in detention or quarantine, some merely waiting until they could be processed, others until officials were satisfied that they met all the requirements for admission.

But fear often was mixed with exhilaration and relief, especially among those who had left behind persecution, extreme poverty, and near starvation in their homeland.

Edward Corsi, who emigrated with his family from Italy in 1907, when he was ten, later described the mixed feelings of the immigrants upon their arrival.

> *My first impressions of the new world will always remain etched in my memory, particularly that hazy October morning when I first saw Ellis Island.*
>
> *The steamer* Florida, *fourteen days out of Naples, filled to capacity with 1,600 natives of Italy, had weathered one of the worst storms in our captain's memory....My mother, my stepfather, my brother Giuseppe, and my two sisters, Liberta and Helvetia, all of us together, happy that we had come through the storm safely, clustered on the foredeck for fear of separation and looked with wonder on this miraculous land of our dreams.*
>
> *Passengers all about us were crowding against the rail. Jabbered conversation, sharp cries, laughs and cheers—a steadily rising din filled the air. Mothers and fathers lifted up the babies so that they too could see, off to the left, the Statue of Liberty...looming shadowy through the mist, it brought silence to the decks of the* Florida.
>
> *This symbol of America, this enormous expression of what we had all been taught was the inner meaning of this new country we were coming to—inspired awe in the hopeful immigrants.*

The euphoria was short-lived, however. As Corsi describes in his 1935 autobiography, *In the Shadow of Liberty*, the immigrants' first steps into America were often less than pleasant. The ship's officers were brusque, if not rude, in readying the passengers for arrival.

OPPOSITE: *Hope and anticipation are plain in the faces of these immigrants as they wait to be transferred to Ellis Island.*

Lewis W. Hine/New York Public Library

ABOVE: *During the peak immigration years, Ellis Island's facilities were so overcrowded that newcomers such as this Italian family might have to wait several days on their ship before a ferry could even bring them to the island.*

Instead of offering kind words as the newcomers prepared to step into a new land, the officers pushed and shoved them, shouted demands, and herded the passengers into groups "as though we were animals."

The Corsis were among the first people off the ocean liner. They boarded a small boat for the brief journey to Ellis Island, and learned later that some of their fellow passengers had to wait several days and nights before being taken ashore.[1]

The Corsis were lucky indeed, for 1907 was the peak year for immigration, with more than one million people landing at Ellis Island. Between five and ten thousand were processed daily by the overworked doctors, clerks, translators, baggage handlers, ticket agents, and food suppliers. Ships that came in when the island was loaded to capacity were forced to keep their third-class passengers on board until the crowds eased, a process that sometimes took days.

First- and second-class passengers did not have to go through this waiting period since they were given a cursory examination aboard ship and allowed to pass directly into New York City. This discrimination against those traveling third class—what had

New York Public Library

Passengers crowded against the rails of the ferry during the brief trip to Ellis Island, eager to glimpse the imposing Statue of Liberty to the south and the awe-inspiring New York skyline to the north.

earlier been steerage—led to some bitterness among the passengers below decks. Hans Bergner, one of those who arrived in 1924, was still indignant about it fifty years later:

> *When we arrived on the 26th of December, on a very, very cold winter day, and the passenger ship was fastened to the pier—Pier 84, I believe it was at the foot of 44th Street in Manhattan—the first-class passengers were asked to leave the ship. The second-class passengers followed. Then the announcement went around—all third-class passengers were please to remain on board overnight. They would be fed on the ship, be given a breakfast the following morning, at which time a lighter would come to take us over to Ellis Island. And so there was this slight feeling among many of us that, "Isn't it strange that here we are coming to a country where there is complete equality, but not quite so for the newly arrived immigrants?"[2]*

Once on Ellis Island, the immigrants typically had many more long waits, and the best they could hope for was a two- to three-hour ordeal. As they entered the main processing hall, they were invited to leave their baggage in storage on the main floor of the building while they went through the inspection process. They carried the identification papers that had been prepared for them when they boarded ship in Europe, and manifest tags referring to their ship were fastened to their clothes.

At the height of immigration, baggage jammed the entire first floor of the Main Building. The anxious looks on the faces of this Italian family are due to lost luggage.

Lewis W. Hine/New York Public Library

Until 1911, all immigrants had to climb a flight of stairs to the second floor examination room, which was 200 feet (60m) long and 100 feet (30m) wide and divided into twelve narrow lanes to keep the lines of immigrants awaiting inspection orderly. Doctors used the stairs as part of the examination process, watching the immigrants as they ascended the stairway to see if they could detect any signs of lameness or other obvious deformities that might disqualify an immigrant.

A group of Slavic immigrants holding precious papers and belongings ascend the stairs to the Registry Room. Doctors at the top carefully observed each person's climb.

Lewis W. Hine/New York Public Library

After 1911, however, the building was remodeled and the entire medical examination was moved to the main floor of the inspection building. An observer in 1913 described the new procedure:

> *When they enter they are lined up in long rows, with two doctors for each row. They must walk down a narrow lane made by rows of piping with an interval of 20 feet (6m) between them. As they approach, the doctors begin to size up each immigrant. First they survey him as a whole. If the general impression is favorable they cast their eyes at his feet to see if they are all right. Then come his legs, his body, his hands, his arms, his face, his eyes, and his head.*
>
> *While the immigrant has been walking the 20 feet (6m), the doctors have asked and answered in their own minds several hundred questions. If the immigrant reveals any intimation of any disease, if he has any deformity, even down to a crooked finger, the fact is noticed.*

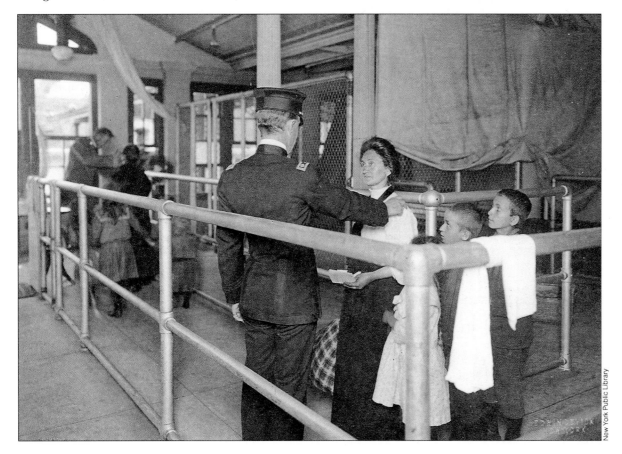

A mother and her children wait for medical examination. At the far left of the photograph, a doctor can be seen checking a child's eyes for signs of trachoma.

New York Public Library

If he is so evidently a healthy person that the examination reveals no reason why he should be held, he is passed on. But if there is the least suspicion in the minds of the doctors that there is anything at all wrong with him, a chalk mark is placed upon the lapel of his coat.[3]

ABOVE, LEFT: *The medical examination was the most dreaded part of the process for many immigrants. Fear and anxiety are plain in the faces of these women as they wait to be examined.*

The chalk marks were coded—B for back, C for conjunctivitis, Ct for trachoma, E for eyes, F for face, Ft for feet, G for goiter, H for heart, K for hernia, L for lameness, N for neck, P for physical and lungs, Pg for pregnancy, Sc for scalp, S for senility, X for mental retardation, and a circled K for insanity. On average, fifteen to twenty percent of the immigrants were marked for further examination.

ABOVE, RIGHT: *A doctor examines a woman who bears a chalk mark on her dress, courtesy of a sharp-eyed inspector.*

One of the most dreaded parts of the physical was the eye examination, in which doctors flipped up the eyelids of each immigrant with a buttonhook, a hairpin, or their fingers, searching for a common eye disease of the time, trachoma, which was common in Southeastern Europe, but relatively unknown in North America. Because the disease was contagious and could lead to blindness if not treated, those found to have trachoma were not allowed to enter the United States. Sometimes, the disease was discovered by inspectors at the point of embarkation. Either way, it was devastating, as the writer Sholom Aleichem described in sketches about his journey to America:

> At Antwerp, waiting for the ship to take us to America, we meet Goldele, a girl with bad eyes. People tell her family to go to the doctor. So they go to the doctor. The doctor examines them and finds they are all hale and hearty and can go to America, but she, Goldele, cannot go because she has trachomas on her eyes. At first her family do not understand. Only later do they realize what it means. It means that they can all go to America but she, Goldele, will have to remain behind in Antwerp. So there begins a wailing, a weeping, a moaning. Three times her mama faints. Her papa wants to stay with her but he can't. All the ship tickets would be lost. So they have to go off to America and leave her, Goldele, here until the trachomas will go away from her eyes.[4]

A book of instructions for medical examiners at Ellis Island warned the doctors that trachoma was prevalent among "Syrians, Greeks, Armenians, Russians, and Finns and that, especially among the latter mentioned race, many cases of trachoma are found which give no outward evidence of the disease." The instruction manual also explained that the purpose of excluding the immigrants who were found to have trachoma was "not only to prevent the introduction into this country of a communicable disease, but also to keep out a class of persons from whom so large a proportion of the inmates of institutions for the blind and recipients of public dispensary charity are recruited."

Favus, a contagious scalp disease that was difficult to cure, also was common among immigrants from southeast Europe and was a cause for deportation as well.

Immigrants who got past the medical inspectors continued down the line and next met a woman whose job it was to look for likely prostitutes. Then the newcomers were divided into groups, according to how they were listed on the ship's manifest, and waited their turn to answer a list of questions—name, age, sex, marital status, occupation, literacy, nationality, last residence, final destination, how the journey was

North Wind Picture Archives

ABOVE: *This unfortunate child suffered from trachoma, a contagious disease of the eyes that was a common cause for rejection.*

OPPOSITE: *In 1907, the peak year of immigration, 13,064 of 1,285,349 immigrants were sent home, most because of disease or the inspector's conclusion that the person in question was likely to become a public charge.*

PENNSTATE

Ogontz Campus

1855

Continuing Education
(215) 886-9450

Favus - a contagious scalp disease - was Cause for deportation

FPG International

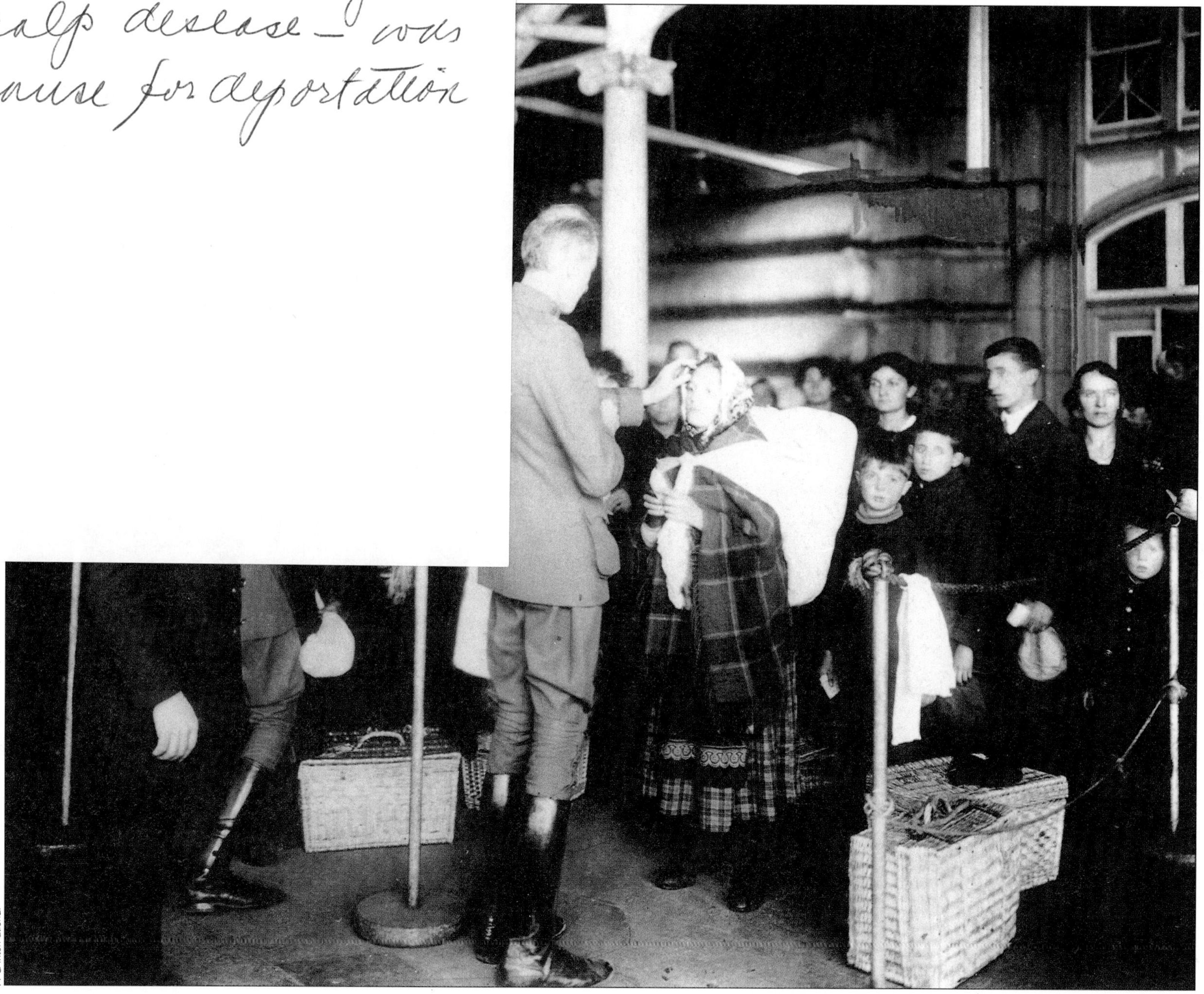

financed, how much money they had, whether they were being met by a relative, whether they had been in the United States before, in prison, in an almshouse, supported by charity, whether a polygamist, if in the United States to do contract labor, and whether deformed or crippled.

The telegraph office helped immigrants to send telegrams to notify relatives of their safe arrival in America.

Although the government provided interpreters to aid the immigrants, there was often much confusion among them at this barrage of questions, especially about names. Inspectors at Ellis Island had to decipher the immigrants' names from handwritten manifest sheets supplied by the ships. The names had been recorded at the port of exit before leaving the country, and many may have been changed or simplified at that point. Helen Barth, who worked for the Hebrew Immigrant Aid Society from

1914 to 1917, described how many people left their homes with one name and arrived in America with another:

> They spoke very badly, were very nervous. The inspector would say, "Where do you come from?" And they would say, "Berlin." The inspector would put the name down 'Berliner.' The name was not Berliner. That's no name.
>
> All the 'witz's and 'ski's got their names from their fathers. For example, Myerson is the son of Myer. We knew that and changed the names here because they were spelled so badly. For instance, a Polish name would be Skyzertski, and they didn't even know how to spell it, so it would be changed to Sanda, to names like that. It was much easier that way.
>
> Then there were names like 'Vladimir.' That would be Walter in American, or Willie, some name like that. Vladimir was strictly a Russian name, you know, and they often were very anxious to Americanize quickly.
>
> And sometimes the children and parents would use first names, and they would call the father 'Adam,' and it became 'Mr. Adam,' and that was the way they went through.[5]

This sad group of Russian orphans—their mothers killed in a massacre in the homeland—arrived in America in 1908.

Fiorello LaGuardia, who served three terms as mayor of New York City beginning in 1933, worked as an interpreter at Ellis Island when he was a young man going to law school, starting in 1907. In his autobiography, *The Making of an Insurgent*, he describes the inspectors' working days:

The work on the island was difficult and strenuous. For two years we worked seven days a week, for immigration was very heavy at this time....Immigrants were pouring in at the average rate of 5,000 a day and it was a constant grind from the moment we got into our uniforms early in the morning until the last minute before we left on the 5:30 boat in the evening. We had to catch the 8:40 ferry every morning.

The immigration laws were rigidly enforced, and there were many heart-breaking scenes on Ellis Island. I never managed during the three years I worked there to become callous to the mental anguish, the disappointment and the despair I witnessed almost daily.[6]

Despair was evident in the faces of those forced to stay overnight or longer on Ellis Island because of physical or mental problems spotted in the initial inspection. In 1911, Sydney Bass, a college-educated Methodist minister from England who was detained because of a bad leg, described the experience to a congressional committee investigating conditions at Ellis Island:

On arriving at Ellis Island the first thing that occurred that gave an indication of what I might expect was the porter putting us in line and calling out: "Get on upstairs, you cattle. You will soon have a nice little pen."...I had my medical examination and I took my certificate, which showed that I had had infantile paralysis of the right leg. I explained to the doctor, facetiously, that I did not preach with my feet, and he said, "All right. You can straighten that out with the immigration authorities...."

After going through the various pens, I arrived at 9:30 in the common room and that is the basis of the bulk of my complaint....There is awful congestion there and it is the height of cruelty to herd people together in such crowded, congested quarters, under such unsani-

ABOVE: *A 1917 photograph of Fiorello La Guardia, who worked as an interpreter at Ellis Island during his years at law school.*

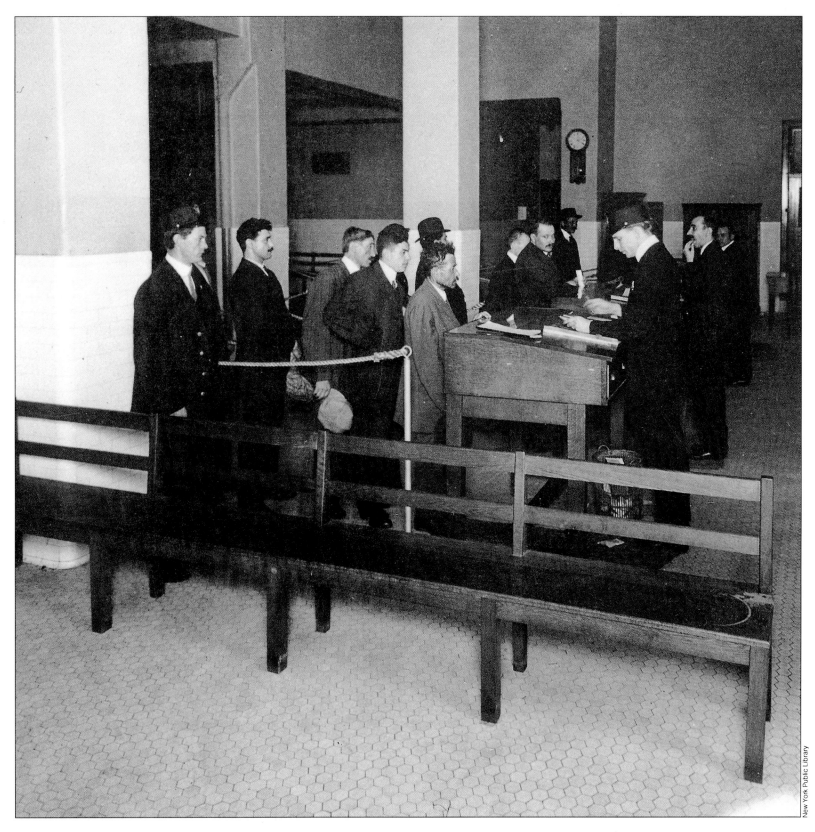

tary conditions, where there is not sufficient air space....I was there on the first day from 9:30 in the morning until 7:30 at night, standing all the time, except occasionally when I sat on the ground...on the second day I was there from 4:20 a.m. til 10:30 a.m. When my name was called I had difficulty in getting out of the crowded room....I had been detained for 28 hours before my case was called at all, after I had specifically stated to the first inspector I met that I was a minister of the gospel, and I had my certificate of successes in examinations and my conference credentials in my possession as well as my property.[7]

LaGuardia said he also saw many cases in which immigrants appeared to be detained unfairly, especially among those classified as mentally deficient. He felt that more than half of those deported for mental problems were wrongly diagnosed, primarily because of a communication failure between doctor and patient.

One case haunted me for years. A young girl in her teens from the mountains of northern Italy turned up at Ellis Island. No one understood her particular dialect very well, and because of her hesitancy in replying to questions she did not understand, she was sent to the hospital for observation. I could imagine the effect on this girl, who had always been carefully sheltered and had never been permitted to be in the company of a man alone, when a doctor suddenly rapped her on the knees, looked into her eyes, turned her on her back and tickled her spine to ascertain her reflexes. The child rebelled—and how! It was the cruelest case I ever witnessed on the island. In two weeks' time that child was a raving maniac, although she had been sound and normal when she arrived at Ellis Island.[8]

After their long journey the immigrants were often bewildered and the general anxiety of the inspection procedure exacerbated their confusion. Despite the presence of interpreters whose job was to ease communication, misunderstandings were common. In this atmosphere, some became hysterical when separated from family members for medical reasons. M. Gertrude Slaughter, an examining physician at the island in the early 1920s, describes one such incident:

ABOVE: *This inspection card, dating from 1911, gives the name of the ship on which the immigrant traveled to America, plus the immigrant's name, point of departure, and last residence.*

OPPOSITE: *Special inquiry rooms were set aside to hear appeals from those immigrants who failed the legal inspection.*

*It was in connection with the hospital that I saw one of the instances in which the attend-
ants were the recipients of blows. Scarlet fever had developed in the child of an immigrant
after the ship had passed quarantine. The parents were well and were directed to the first
island, while the orderlies came with a
stretcher to take the child to the contagious ward. Immediately the mother
attacked the attendants, beating and
scratching them, and then tried to throw
herself into the bay because she thought
her child was being taken from her forever.
Another attendant then had to hold the
mother gently but firmly until an interpreter could be found who spoke her language; he explained the situation
thoroughly, and peace was restored.*[9]

Throughout the prime years of immigration, the highest numbers of arrivals
were rejected because of disease or
because the inspectors had concluded
they were likely to become a public charge. In 1907, the peak year of immigration,
there were 13,064 sent home out of 1,285,349 immigrants.

Because Ellis Island was such an intense and often traumatic experience, some immigrants never discussed the ordeal with their children. New York Governor Mario
Cuomo, whose mother, Immaculata, arrived at Ellis Island in 1927 with her infant son
Frank to meet her husband, says she seldom mentioned the experience to her children
because, "It wasn't always a happy memory." These sentiments are no doubt shared by
many others who passed through Ellis Island.

The experience left some wondering if the trip had been worthwhile. Dutch writer
David Cornel De Jong recalled how he felt as a twelve-year-old arriving in 1917:

*A leaf-strewn corridor in the
contagious disease wards of the
Hospital Building on Island 2
reveals the state of decay into
which most of the buildings on
Ellis Island had fallen after the
island was abandoned.*

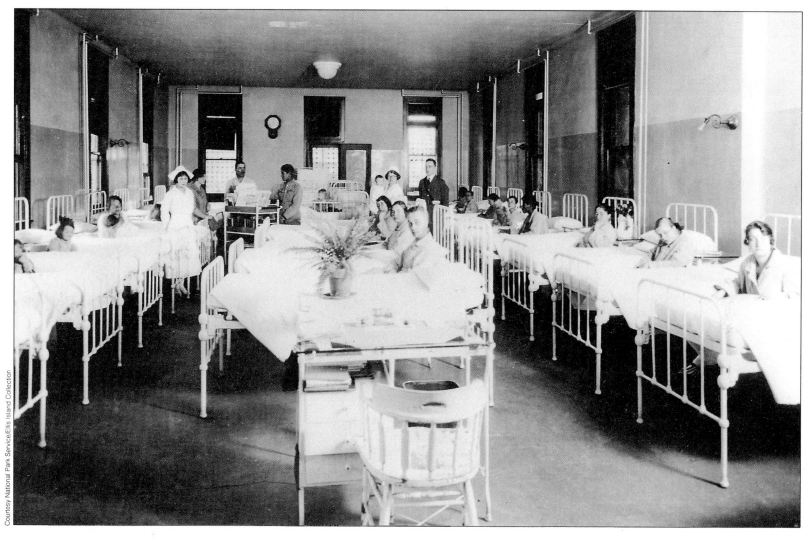

How could it be, I wondered, that after having been so impatient to get there, I suddenly seemed almost frightened by America now that we had arrived. Was it because our uncertain future was only becoming concrete and unescapable, and that uncertainty had to become part and parcel of me like any previous actuality?…We had left home behind; we were not approaching a new home, only an indefinite spot in an unknown vacuum…and even if our early hopes had lasted for a few hours, the miseries of Ellis Island would have wiped them out efficiently.…We were shunted here and there, handled and mishandled, kicked about and torn apart, in a way no farmer would allow his cattle to be treated. "From here on," Father predicted with some strange foresight, "We are no longer men created in the image of God, but less than dumb beasts."[10]

During the peak years of immigration, Ellis Island's hospital beds were often filled. The contagious disease wards frequently cared for children suffering from measles, scarlet fever, diptheria, and other illnesses.

But for all the sad experiences on Ellis Island, eighty percent of the arrivals passed through with little trouble and were rewarded at the end of the day by a long-awaited reunion with relatives and friends. Edward Corsi, the young Italian who arrived at Ellis Island in 1907, went back as the immigration commissioner in the 1930s, when the heyday of immigration was over. He interviewed Frank Martocci, who had been an inspector on the island in 1907, about some of the happy scenes. Martocci recalled them fondly: "Very often brides came over to marry here, and of course we had to act as witnesses. I have no count, but I'm sure I must have helped at hundreds and hundreds of weddings of all nationalities and all types. The weddings were numberless, until they dropped the policy of marrying them at the island and brought them to City Hall in New York." He adds:

> *Incidentally, you may have heard, there is a post at Ellis Island which through long usage has come to earn the name of 'The Kissing Post.' It is probably the spot of greatest interest on the island, and if the immigrants recall it afterward it is always, I am sure, with fondness. For myself, I found it a real joy to watch some of the tender scenes that took place there.*
>
> *There was a line of desks where the inspectors stood with their backs towards the windows and facing the wall. Further back, behind a partition, the witnesses (friends and relatives) waited outside for the detained aliens. As the aliens were brought out, the witnesses were brought in to be examined as to their rights of claim. If the inspector found no hitch, they were allowed to join each other. This, because of the arrangement of the partitions, usually took place at 'The Kissing Post,' where friends, sweethearts, husbands and wives, parents and children would embrace and kiss and shed tears for pure joy.*[11]

OPPOSITE: *The wooden railings in the restored special inquiry rooms were built using a small piece of the original railing.*

BELOW: *Between 1820 and 1978, 3,374,000 Russians emigrated to America, among them this hopeful-looking family who arrived at Ellis Island in 1905.*

New York Public Library

ABOVE: *Clutching manifest tags given to them on the ship that brought them to America, a line of immigrants waits for admission to the Main Building.*

MAINTENANCE
RAILROAD TICKETS
RELEASE OFFICE

SOCIAL SERVICES
VISITOR'S ROOM
ROOMS NO. MW & ME 200 to 249

© Brian Feeney

Writer Louis Adamic, who arrived at Ellis Island in 1913, described in his autobiography the relief many immigrants like him must have felt when they got through the process in a short time. An inspector had confused Adamic's papers and accused him of lying, of declaring another immigrant named Steve Radin to be his uncle, when in fact they were not even acquainted. After several minutes, however, the clerk discovered his mistake "and, waving his hand in a casual gesture, he ordered me released.…I was weak in the knees and just managed to walk out of the room, then downstairs and onto the ferryboat. I had been shouted at, denounced as a liar by an official of the United States on my second day in the country, before a roomful of people, including Steve Radin, whom, so far, I had merely glimpsed."

Adamic continues, "But the weakness in my knees soon passed. I laughed, perhaps a bit hysterically, as the little Ellis Island ferryboat bounded over the rough, white-capped waters of the bay toward the Battery. Steve Radin gaped at me. Then he smiled. I was in New York—in America."[12]

LEFT: *Amid the destruction wrought by time and weather stand the remnants of a sign that once directed immigrants to the next step of their journey.*

BELOW: *Stuck in a kind of limbo as they waited to be accepted or rejected, the immigrants must have looked with longing at the island of Manhattan, at once so close and yet unreachable.*

New York Public Library

Many of those who entered the country via Ellis Island in one way or another contributed to the greatness of America. A few of the more famous examples are listed below.

Name	Home Land	Year	Career
Irving Berlin (1888–1989)	Russia	1892	Songwriter
Knute Rockne (1888–1931)	Norway	1893	Football Coach
Felix Frankfurter (1882–1965)	Austria	1894	Supreme Court Justice
Al Jolson (1886–1950)	Russia	1894	Actor, Singer, Songwriter
Samuel Goldwyn (1881–1974)	Poland	1896	Film Industry Mogul
Pauline Newman (1894–1986)	Lithuania	1901	Labor Leader
Edward G. Robinson (1893–1973)	Rumania	1903	Actor
Frank Capra (1897–)	Italy	1903	Movie Director
Edward Flanagan (1886–1948)	Ireland	1903	Priest; Founder of Boy's Town

Many of the immigrants who passed through Ellis Island went on to achieve great success in America. For example, David Dubinsky (OPPOSITE PAGE, FAR LEFT), who came from Russia at the age of 19, went on to become one of America's most important labor leaders. Norwegian-born Knute Rockne (OPPOSITE PAGE, RIGHT), the football coach who inspired his team to "win one for the Gipper," came through Ellis Island in 1893. Irving Berlin (LEFT), the prolific composer of such classics as God Bless America, White Christmas, and Annie Get Your Gun, was born in Russia, and passed through Ellis Island in 1892. Felix Frankfurter (BELOW), Justice of the Supreme Court from 1939 to 1962, came from Austria in 1894.

Name	Home Land	Year	Career
Bob Hope (1903–)	England	1908	Comedian
David Dubinsky (1892–1982)	Russia	1911	Labor Leader
Bela Lugosi (1882–1956)	Hungary	1921	Actor
Isaac Asimov (1920–)	Russia	1923	Scientist-Author

The Industrial Revolution, which eventually brought a new prosperity to Europe, initially caused many people to lose their jobs—and created a boom in immigration to America.

THE OLD COUNTRY

CHAPTER FIVE

FPG International

Immigrants came to America for many reasons—to escape war, famine, religious persecution, political upheaval, lack of jobs; for fear of conscription, family disagreements, personal failure, and lust for adventure. What was most shared was the hope for a better life, not only financially, but also emotionally and spiritually, a place where they could escape the rigid class structures and religious restrictions of Europe and find new opportunities and freedoms for themselves and their children.

In the hundred years after 1820 it is estimated that fifty-five million people emigrated from Europe, most of them to North America. As mentioned earlier, until the late 1800s, the bulk of immigrants to the United States came from England, Ireland, and Germany, with substantial numbers from the Scandinavian countries as well.

As historian Samuel Eliot Morison noted in *The Oxford History of the American People*, the number of immigrants who came to America in the nineteenth century was so large in relation to the population that they transformed the country. In the 1820s there were 129,000 immigrants; by the 1830s there were 540,000, of whom 44 percent were Irish, 30 percent German, and 15 percent English. That figure almost tripled in the 1840s and rose to 2.8 million in the 1850s. About half the immigrants in the 1840s were Irish, and many of the rest Germans.

At the same time, the U.S. population grew from 9.6 million in 1820 to 12.9 million in 1830, 17 million in 1840, 23.2 million in 1850, and 31.5 million in 1860.

From Ireland alone, 3.8 million immigrants arrived between the mid-1800s and the end of America's Open Door policy in the 1920s. This huge migration is attributed in large part to a system of land ownership and commercialization of agriculture that Britain imposed on Ireland, ultimately making it almost impossible for the peasants to survive. During the mid-1800s, while other countries were developing large urban populations, Ireland remained more than 80 percent rural, with many farmers earning only a subsistence living. As the population grew, the situation worsened.

Between 1845 and 1855, Ireland suffered a famine caused by successive failures of the potato crop, which provided in most cases the only food for the country's peasants. In August 1846, Father Theobald Matthew, traveling from Dublin to Cork, observed fields of potatoes blighted with a fungus that struck without warning and made potatoes inedible. "In many places," he wrote, "the wretched people were seated on the fences of their decaying gardens, wringing their hands and wailing bitterly the destruction that had left them foodless."[1]

Relief efforts were sporadic and hampered by the English belief—succinctly expressed by the English director of government relief, Charles Trevelyan, in 1845— that the problem in Ireland was not famine, but "the selfish, perverse and turbulent character of the people."[2]

By 1847, however, so many had died of starvation that two thousand relief committees were distributing free food to more than three million people—40 percent of the population. It is estimated that more than one million died of starvation or related diseases. In the north midlands, in 1846, a visitor reported "sights that will never wholly leave the eyes that beheld them, cowering wretches almost naked in the savage weather, prowling in turnip fields and endeavouring to grub up roots...little children ...their limbs fleshless, their faces bloated yet wrinkled and of a pale greenish hue, who would never, it was too plain, grow up to be men and women."[3]

During this period, the British continued to export food from the starving land to England. Irish landlords also took advantage of the famine to evict famished tenants and consolidate their landholdings. In 1847, Parliament did the landholders a favor by forbidding public relief to any head of household who held a quarter-acre or more of land and refused to give it up. Wives and children of the holdout farmers were also frequently denied food. It is estimated that half a million or more were evicted between 1846 and 1855.

During this period 2.1 million Irish—one-fourth the pre-famine population—left their homeland, with 1.5 million sailing to the United States.

It was also a turbulent time for the rest of Europe. In 1847, farmers rioted in France, and there were uprisings over shortages of bread and potatoes in Germany. Count Galen, the Prussian minister, wrote in January 1847, "The old year ended in scarcity, the new one opens with starvation. Misery, spiritual and physical, traverses Europe in ghastly shapes—the one without God, the other without bread. Woe if they join hands."[4]

FPG International

The agricultural failures in Europe came in tandem with a widespread economic depression that halted industrial expansion and led to substantial unemployment and unrest in the cities. In 1848 King Louis-Philippe of France was overthrown in Paris, and the news spurred a series of sympathetic revolutions in the German confederation. That year there also were unsuccessful revolutions in Italy and Austria-Hungary. Several thousand of the political unfortunates set sail for America, where they hoped to find freedom and a better life.

Germany alone sent 1.5 million immigrants to the United States in the four decades before the Civil War, a great many of them craftsmen who could not compete with the factories that sprung up with the Industrial Revolution, and farmers, who were squeezed off their land by large-scale producers. Similar changes were responsible for smaller numbers of English and Scandinavian immigrants leaving Europe during this period.

Gjert Hovland, a Norwegian immigrant who settled in New York, was typical of those who wrote to friends and relatives at home in the 1830s about the economic opportunities America offered:

> *We have gained more since our arrival here than I did during all the time I lived in Norway and I have every prospect of earning a living here for myself and my family—even if my family becomes larger—so long as God gives me good health.*
>
> *Such excellent plans have been developed here that, even though one be infirm, no one need go hungry. Competent men are elected to see that no needy persons, either in the cities or in the country, shall have to beg. If a man dies and leaves a widow and children who are unable to support themselves—as often happens—they have the privilege of petitioning these officials. Each one will then receive every year as much clothing and food as he needs, and no discrimination is shown between the native born and those from foreign countries. These things I have learned through daily observation.*[5]

Letters such as these were passed from friend to friend and village to village and spurred great interest in immigration. In addition, western states, desperate for development and hungry for more population, distributed booklets describing their land, crops, wages, and climate. Shipping agents and ethnic societies lured Europeans to the New World as well.

Another factor that led to increased immigration was the changing attitude of European governments, which until the early nineteenth century had opposed and even banned immigration for skilled workers who were needed at home. Between 1750 and 1850, however, the population of Europe doubled, and overcrowding became a concern. By the 1830s, England no longer discouraged those who wanted to leave—even those who were well trained—and the number of British immigrants swelled over the next five decades, rising from 32,000 in the 1840s to 247,000 in the 1850s to a peak of 644,000 in the 1880s.

Germany was somewhat slower to ease its restrictive laws. In 1836, the American counsel at Bremen reported: "The different governments of Germany are, in general, not much pleased with the spirit of immigration…and as is said, try by all means to keep their subjects at home. The immigrants often loudly and bitterly complain that the said governments, before they give to people permission to depart, put as many obstacles as possible in their way."[6]

After the thwarted 1848 revolution, however, German leaders shifted their stance, making emigration considerably easier. The changing character of the German Confederation also led many to seek escape from the military and an industrial depression in the 1880s led to a large exodus of skilled craftsmen—coalminers, iron and steelworkers, weavers, spinners, glassworkers, and leather workers.

Norway, Sweden, and Switzerland were all suffering from overpopulation by the middle of the nineteenth century, and immigration was never discouraged.

These early steelworkers were part of the Industrial Revolution, which sent many farmers and craftsmen who could no longer compete in Europe's changing markets to America.

In 1882, the American economy was on an upswing, and immigration rose to an unprecedented 788,000, of whom 250,000 were German, 179,000 British and Irish, and 105,000 Scandinavian. These countries—Ireland, Germany, Britain, and the Scandinavian nations—continued to dominate immigration to the United States until about 1890. After this point, immigration from these parts of Europe fell off sharply, partly because of domestic land reforms designed to entice people to remain in the Mother Country and also because of improving opportunities in industry.

The so-called "old" immigrants were replaced by "new" immigrants who came primarily from southern and eastern Europe. Between 1890 and 1914, fifteen million people came to the United States, most of them from Austria-Hungary, Russia, Italy, Greece, Romania, and Turkey.

The new immigrants came for much the same reason as the old ones had—economic opportunity. Many fell victim to the same changing land policies and agricultural dislocations that had occurred earlier in northern and western Europe, policies that turned them from small-time farmers into unskilled laborers.

OPPOSITE: Factories in Germany, such as the Krupp works pictured here, suffered from an industrial depression that hit Europe in the 1880s, leading to a surge in emigration to America.

Religious persecution forced many people to leave their homelands in hope of finding freedom and success in the United States.

New York Public Library

This change occurred first in the Austro-Hungarian empire, where land was sub-divided into such tiny plots that the peasants could not make a living on them. In Italy, chronic poverty grew even worse in the 1880s because of a French tariff against Italian wines and competition for Italian fruits from Florida and California.

Russian immigrants came for different reasons, primarily political and religious. The largest numbers were Jews, who, after the assassination of Czar Alexander II in 1881, fell victim to increasingly brutal policies. In 1882, restrictions were placed on Jewish worship, and Jews were excluded from holding public office and from many professions. Most were forced to move to an area bordering Germany, Austria, and Romania, called the Pale of Settlement. Large numbers of Jews were massacred in the pograms of 1881-82, 1891, and 1905-6.

Mary Antin, a Russian Jew who came to the United States in the 1890s, wrote about the pograms in her autobiography, *The Promised Land.*

After the assassination of Czar Alexander II (ABOVE) in 1881, Russian Jews became the victims of widespread persecution and brutal pograms. Many escaped to America.

OPPOSITE: *New York City's Lower East Side was home to large numbers of Jewish immigrants, who imparted to the area the unique flavor that it retains to this day.*

> *The Passover season, when we celebrated our deliverance from the land of Egypt, and felt so glad and thankful, as if it had only just happened, was the time our Gentile neighbors chose to remind us that Russia was another Egypt. That is what I heard people say, and it was true. It was not so bad in Polotzk, within the Pale; but in Russian cities and even more in the country districts, where Jewish families lived scattered, by special permission of the police, who were always changing their minds about letting them stay, the Gentiles made the Passover a time of horror for the Jews.*
>
> *Somebody would start up that lie about murdering Christian children and the stupid peasants would get mad about it, and fill themselves with vodka and set out to kill the Jews. They attacked them with knives and clubs and scythes and axes, killed them or tortured them and burned their houses. This was called a pogrom.*
>
> *Jews who escaped the pograms came to Polotzk with wounds on them and horrible, horrible stories, of little babies torn limb from limb before their mothers' eyes. Only to hear these things made one sob and sob and choke with pain. People who saw such things never*

Chronic poverty led many Italians to seek a better life across the ocean. This Italian family opened a grocery in New York City's "Little Italy."

smiled any more, no matter how long they lived; and sometimes their hair turned white in a day, and some people became insane on the spot.[7]

With the start of the pograms, large numbers of Jews left Russia. In 1880, five thousand Russian Jews emigrated to the United States. That number rose to 81,000 by 1892 and peaked at 258,000 in 1907.

While Jews constituted the majority of Russian immigrants before the turn of the century, they were joined after 1900 by substantial number of Poles, Finns, Lithuanians, and Russo-Germans.

These three countries—Austria-Hungary, Italy, and Russia—were the primary sources of "new" immigrants coming to the United States after 1890, a fact that displeased large numbers of "old" immigrants who felt threatened by the ethnic background of the newcomers.

The annual report of U.S. Treasury Secretary William Windom in 1891 described the changes: "The arrivals during the first four months of the present fiscal year have been 189,788, an excess of 40,595, or of more than 27 percent over the corresponding months of 1890. This extraordinary and progressive increase in the tide of alien immigration to the United States…has not failed to attract the attention of the whole country, and it will doubtless command the early consideration of Congress." The report also reflected the fears of some Americans: "An analysis of the statement of arrivals during the last fiscal year shows that an increasing proportion of immigrants is coming to us from those classes and those countries of Europe whose people are least adapted to, and least prepared for, citizenship in a free republic, and are least inclined to assimilate with the general body of American citizens."[8]

Over the next few years, several proposals were presented before Congress to limit immigration. All failed except for new provisions designed to keep out people with contagious diseases and to make the shipping companies assume more responsibility for the immigrants transported to America.

But the fears of 1891 were only a harbinger of the anti-immigrant mania that later would sweep the country and lead to "Deportation Delirium."

An embarkation card from the Red Star Line for a passenger traveling from Antwerp.

The chief sources of American immigration from 1820 to 1978 (from *American Heritage* magazine):			
Country of Origin	**Total Immigrants**	**Percent of Total**	**Peak Year**
Germany	6,978,000	14.3	1882
Italy	5,294,000	10.9	1907
Britain	4,898,000	10.01	1888
Ireland	4,723,000	9.7	1851
Austria-Hungary	4,315,000	8.9	1907
Canada	4,105,000	8.4	1924
Russia	3,374,000	6.9	1913
Scandinavia	2,525,000	5.2	1882

During World War I, enemy aliens around the country were arrested.
These men are Germans arriving at Hoboken station from Fort
Oglethorpe, Georgia, where they had been interned. From Hoboken,
they went to Ellis Island to be deported.

DEPORTATION DELIRIUM

CHAPTER SIX

FPG International

Immigration fell dramatically during World War I, dropping from 1.2 million in 1914 to 326,700 in 1915, a reduction of 75 percent. The number of arrivals processed through Ellis Island was down as well, from 878,052 in 1914 to 178,416 the following year. With a smaller staff headed by an administrator who endeavored to end its unfortunate reputation as the "Isle of Tears," Ellis Island was to experience a much-needed rejuvenation of spirit.

Frederick Howe, appointed to the job by President Woodrow Wilson in 1914, came into office full of enthusiasm and reformer's zeal. He was a friend of Wilson's and had been a law professor at Cooper Union

Lewis Hine/New York Public Library

in New York City. He set about at once making life more comfortable for the immigrants, especially those who were detained for long periods with nothing to do but sit in pens all day, men on one side, women and children on another.

Lawns that had heretofore been off limits to immigrants were put to good use. Benches and play areas were constructed and became popular gathering places. A classroom was set up for children and teachers recruited to teach them; needlework lessons were offered for women and calisthenics and athletic games for men.

"Some of these peasants had been away from the soil, shut up indoors, for months," Howe said. "It meant a lot to them to get out into the sunlight and feel the grass under their feet again." Howe's humanitarian changes did not end there, however:

> *The next step was to find a common hall, that families might be together every day. As long as the warm weather lasts, the enclosed porch overlooking the city makes a capital social room. They have magazines and pictures here to look at and excellent concerts every Sunday, besides a gramophone to play cheerful tunes for them. Now we want to take down the wire netting from around the examination rooms, which makes them feel like animals in a cage, and then we'll hang maps and pictures on the walls.*

> *The only thing that is lacking over here is imagination. No one ever seemed to try to imagine what a detained immigrant must be feeling.*[1]

These reforms were initially welcomed, or at least drew little vocal opposition. But as Howe noted in his autobiography, *Confessions of a Reformer*, he eventually made powerful enemies.

Second-class passengers at this time were landed directly in Hoboken, New Jersey, and Howe contended they were regularly fleeced upon landing by the usual assortment of petty thieves that gathered around immigrants. He felt they would be safer landing at Ellis Island and proposed a change. An uproar ensued, from both the commercial interests in Hoboken and immigrants who would rather face the con men in New Jersey than the strict inspectors on Ellis Island. Howe lost.

He also had fights with the railroad pools that controlled transportation for immigrants, and he earned the enmity of the steamship lines by increasing the charges they had to pay for detained aliens.

New York Public Library

A typical noontime dinner in 1906 consisted of beef stew, boiled potatoes, and rye bread. Women and children were given crackers and milk, as well. In 1911, a kosher kitchen was added.

One of his biggest battles occurred in 1916, when he succeeded in convincing the government to take over the food concession at Ellis Island. The company that held the food contract put forth a strong objection. The firm's former lawyer, New York Congressman William Bennet, denounced Howe in Washington, calling him "a half-

OPPOSITE: At the Railroad Ticket Office, newcomers happy to have passed the inspections bought tickets to travel on from Ellis Island.

Lewis Hine/New York Public Library

baked radical who has free-love ideas" because he allowed men and women to socialize in an outdoor recreation area at Ellis Island and provided humane treatment of the "anarchists" and "radicals" detained during the war.

This attack foreshadowed the tone many members of Congress would take against the commissioner in the following years.

Although immigration was down, Ellis Island nonetheless maintained a sizeable population because President Woodrow Wilson in 1915 had ordered that no aliens would be deported while Europe was at war. When the United States entered the war in April 1917, seamen on German and Austrian ships in the harbors of New York and New London, Connecticut, were captured and sent to Ellis Island—about 1,150 in all. Other enemy aliens arrested around the country joined them in the months that followed, although they eventually were shipped to internment camps in Hot Springs, North Carolina, and Fort Oglethorpe, Georgia.

By early 1918, the Army Medical Department had taken over the hospital on Ellis Island to treat wounded servicemen, and the Navy used its buildings to quarter men

28939

EDWIN LEVICK
NEW YORK

awaiting ship assignments. During this period, immigrants arriving in New York harbor received medical inspections aboard ship or on the piers. Thousands of people—28,867 to be exact—passed through Ellis Island in 1918.

The military services left Ellis Island in 1919, but it soon filled up again with victims of the "Red Scare" that swept the country at the end of the war. The 2,483 people arrested under a 1918 law that called for excluding anarchists and anyone advocating the overthrow of the government were processed at Ellis Island. The law also allowed for expulsion of "those affiliated with any organization teaching the foregoing views." It was a time when radical, or even different, opinions were dangerous.

Many of those arrested were members of the Socialist-dominated Industrial Workers of the World and the fledgling Communist Party. Strikes by the IWW, or "Wobblies," after the war contributed to the general hysteria, as did newspaper headlines.

Despite public sentiment against the union members and the radicals, Commissioner Howe was outraged at many of the arrests, complaining that he had become a jailer to men who had not been convicted of any crime.

He especially objected to the way many of the radicals were treated.

> *They were brought under guards and in special trains with instructions to get them away from the country with as little delay as possible. Most of the aliens had been picked up in raids on labor headquarters; they had been given a drum-head trial by an inspector with no chance for defense; they were held incommunicado and often were not permitted to see either friends or attorneys, before being shipped to Ellis Island.*
>
> *In these proceedings the inspector who made the arrest was prosecutor, witness, judge, jailer, and executioner. He was clerk and interpreter as well. This was all the trial the alien could demand under the law....I was advised by the commissioner-general to mind my own business and carry out orders, no matter what they might be. Yet such obvious injustice was being done that I could not sit quiet.[2]*

Howe's position was increasingly unpopular, however, and he was strongly denounced in the spring of 1919 for presiding over a rally in Madison Square Garden protesting a food blockade of Russia. He spent that summer at the Paris peace talks to end the

war. When he returned, he found that Commissioner-General Andrew Caminetti had countermanded his order that aliens be given hearings before deportation.

The very next morning he was in Washington at the Department of Labor, exploding in anger at Caminetti. But even as he shouted, Howe said, he knew what the outcome would be: "I was through."

Howe resigned in September 1919. Two months later, the House Committee on Immigration and Naturalization held hearings and revealed that of 697 aliens arrested and sent to Ellis Island for deportation since early 1919, only 60 had actually been deported. Howe was blamed for this, and when he tried to present a defense during the hearings by cross-examining witnesses, he was ejected from the hearing room.

An editorial in the *Cleveland News* captured the general tone of the feelings that ran so strongly against the commissioner. It charged that Ellis Island under Howe had "turned into a Socialist hall, a spouting-ground for Red revolutionists, a Monte Carlo for foreigners only, a club where Europe's offscourings are entertained at American expense...a place of deceit and sham to which foreign mischief-makers are sent temporarily to make the public think the government is courageously deporting them."[3]

A month later the Army transport *Buford* sailed from New York to Finland, carrying 246 men and three women, including the famous revolutionary Emma Goldman. Most of them, members of the Union of Russian Workers, had been treated roughly by the guards at Ellis Island. The night they were deported they were pulled from their beds and marched between rows of soldiers to the cutter. They were not told where they were going.

Emma Goldman (1869-1940), the fiery anarchist writer and activist, was arrested in 1916 for distributing birth control information, then again in 1917 for opposing the draft. She was held at Ellis Island before being deported in 1919.

FPG International

FPG International

This shabby treatment drew criticism later, especially since wives and children were left behind. Louis Post, who was assistant secretary of labor during this period, recalled the problems of the families left behind: "Most of the women whose husbands were thus secretly shipped away from them were dependent upon their husbands for support. Some had saved, out of scant wages for hard work, a little money 'against a rainy day;' but the money of all was beyond their reach, mostly in postal-savings or bank accounts subject to their husbands' drafts or in the form of unpaid wages. Many had sold their household goods, expecting to go along with their husbands. Some had small children to care for. Most of them were in abject want."[4]

The arrests continued the following year. On January 4, 1920, *The New York Times* reported: "With 500 foreign-born members of the Communist Party on Ellis Island at midnight and more than 2,500 others held elsewhere for deportation, the torch of the

Red revolution in America burned low last night." *The Times* described their fate in these terms: "The Communist Party formed at Chicago on Sept. 1 with the confident hopes of bringing about a revolution in the early days of this year which would make the United States a sister state to Soviet Russia was divided into three branches yesterday. One wing was homeward bound on the Soviet *Ark*, the center was being held for embarkation on the *Red Fleet*, which will leave during the month, probably about Saturday, and the rest were in hiding."[5]

Hundreds more aliens were deported in the months that followed, but Post, standing in for the ailing secretary of labor, began to curb the excesses of Commissioner-General Caminetti, insisting on a review of each case scheduled for deportation.

The Red Scare abated as the year wore on and the rooms at Ellis Island that had been used as holding pens emptied. But they filled up just as quickly with new arrivals, for with the end of World War I, immigration was once again on the rise.

OPPOSITE: After World War I, immigration rose rapidly, and Ellis Island, ill-equipped to handle the influx, was once again overwhelmed—line-ups and waits were longer than ever.

Ferries such as this one usually brought hopeful newcomers to Ellis Island, but during the "red scare," also ferried many soon-to-be-deported radicals out to the ships that would take them away from America.

Post-war immigrants were checked much more strictly for diseases.
Here, a group of policemen wait at the Battery for a shipment of
immigrants from Ellis Island who must be tested for typhus.

REVIVAL AND RESTRICTION

World War I turned millions of Europeans into refugees, and many set their sights on a better life in the United States. From a low of 26,731 in 1919, immigration through Ellis Island rose to 225,206 in 1920 and to 560,971 in 1921.

The island, understaffed and in need of major repairs, was ill-equipped to handle the new arrivals, and the country was in no mood to welcome them. The war had left many Americans with a distaste for Europe, and Congress was not inclined to spend money improving the country's chief receiving station.

Immigrants by this time went through a much more rigorous medical inspection than those who had arrived

Medical facilities at Ellis Island were located in a fifteen-building complex, which included laboratories and x-ray facilities, plus hospital beds. In 1924, the peak year of immigration, between forty and fifty surgical procedures were performed there daily.

a decade earlier; they also were tested for literacy. As a result, inspectors were able to process only two thousand a day, less than half the number that had moved through the station on a busy day before the war. Many immigrants were forced to spend an extra day or two aboard ship waiting their turn to be processed.

It was even worse for those who failed to pass the initial inspection. At any one time, thousands were being detained on Ellis Island in what newspapers of the time called disgraceful conditions—a shortage of beds, dirty and inadequate baths and toilets, vermin-infested dormitories, and a staff that was overwhelmed and underpaid.

Greta Wagner, a German woman who went through Ellis Island in 1923, recalled what it was like to arrive in America during this period as a young, single woman without money.

We were shipped first to Ellis Island and that was not very pleasant. It was rough, very rough. Years ago, they called it a cattle farm. Oh, it was just like a barn. Millions of people

New York Public Library

As the flood of immigrants increased, the kitchens were forced to serve meals all day to men, women, and children crowded into the confines of the dining rooms.

standing around with the bundles. You were with a big herd. And they fed us with a wagon full of that cattle food. They slapped it on the plates.

You were just like a number. Over 5,000 a day were arriving from all over—Russia, Romania, Poland, from Germany, from France, and naturally I couldn't speak one word of English....I was detained for two weeks. I talked with the directors every day but I couldn't explain anything. But they wouldn't let me go. They wanted to send me back to Germany...nobody got off of Ellis Island unless they were called for by someone who would stand good for them. Somebody had to come up and sign.[1]

Greta Wagner was saved from deportation by a Catholic charity that guaranteed she would not become a public charge, promising to give her room and board until she could find a job to support herself. A number of different ethnic and religious aid societies intervened on behalf of the immigrants this way frequently, helping thousands of would-be Americans to avoid deportation.

Frederick Wallis, who served as commissioner of Ellis Island for a little more than a year in 1920 and 1921, agreed with the critics that the station was a miserable place but did not succeed in getting money to improve it.

Instead, in 1921, Congress imposed the first quota law on immigration, limiting the number of Europeans who could enter each year to 3 percent of the foreign-born people of that nationality living in the United States in 1910. Only 20 percent of each nation's quota could enter in any month.

This resulted in a mad, uncontrolled rush by the steamship companies to land as many immigrants as possible early each month. Later arrivals often were turned back. Wallis, in a letter to Labor Secretary James Davis, recommended as he left office that the inspection process be transferred from Ellis Island to American consulates overseas, so those rejected would not have to make a heart-breaking journey back across the ocean:

"I do believe," Wallis said, "that our nation is committing a gross injustice for which some day it must render an account, in allowing these hundreds of thousands of people to sell all they have, sever all connections, come 4,000 miles out of the heart of Europe and other countries, only to find after passing the Statue of Liberty that they must go back to the country whence they came."[2]

Wallis was succeeded in October 1921 by Robert Tod, a New York banker who proved to be a good administrator. Under his leadership, some of the corruption that periodically broke out at Ellis Island was cleaned up, and physical improvements were made, but the essential problems of understaffing and general dilapidation remained.

OPPOSITE: As ever-growing numbers of immigrants looked hopefully toward America and the promise of a new life, Americans themselves were becoming increasingly reluctant to allow immigration to continue unrestricted.

Courtesy National Park Service/Ellis Island Collection

ABOVE: By the mid-1920s, Ellis Island was staffed by over 700 overworked interpreters, doctors, nurses, clerks, matrons, maintenance workers, and watchmen.

While Tod was in office, the British ambassador to the United States, Sir Auckland Geddes, was invited to pay a visit to Ellis Island. His subsequent report complimented Tod's efforts, but, like many others who had viewed the conditions there, he was upset by the dirt and overcrowding. Geddes was particularly disturbed by the plight of the detained immigrants, who often had to wait weeks to find out whether the secretary of labor had approved their appeal, or whether they would be deported.

"I feel profoundly sorry," Geddes said, "for some of the temporarily detained, a mother waiting for a delayed child, or a father with his children anxiously watching for his wife to come to him....It is no one's fault and cannot be avoided, unless immigrants to the United States are to be finally approved for admission in their own land before they set out upon their journey."

Geddes commented on the difficulties experienced by the detainees: "Large numbers of the immigrants have to go before a board to determine whether or not they may be admitted....This arrangement, the theory of which is probably right, is in practice nothing short of diabolic. For days some wretched creature is kept in suspense...days slip by into weeks sometimes before a decision is reached....If the United States government will expedite the decision of appeals so that the results can be announced within 24 hours of the completed collection of the facts, the anguish of Ellis Island will be appreciably reduced."[3]

Geddes' report received a lot of attention, and along with other criticisms, eventually led to substantial changes at Ellis Island. Many were made during the administration of Tod's successor, Henry Curran, a New York City Republican who had served as president of the borough of Manhattan.

Curran was determined to improve the treatment the immigrants received. In his memoir, *Pillar to Post*, he described one of his frequent battles with Congress to get money for improvements on Ellis Island.

This Armenian Jew fled Turkish persecution to freedom in America in 1926.

OPPOSITE: *A new American pledges his loyalty.*

He noted that while there were beds in some of the small detention rooms, sleeping quarters in the main hall consisted of wire cages, and that was where 2,000 immigrants slept each night.

Despite the lack of beds, Curran said, there were bedbugs galore, and it took two months to exterminate them. It took two years to get real beds in place of the cages. After visiting Washington repeatedly, Curran finally convinced a couple of congressmen to make the journey to Ellis Island and stretch out on the cages.

"Then the wheels began to turn," he said. "Those congressmen were flaming missionaries for beds instead of cages."[4]

Curran, who served as commissioner of Ellis Island for three years, also was upset by the increasingly strict quota laws he had to enforce. In his memoir, he recalled how he encountered the problem his first day on the job, July 1, 1923:

> *At 6 the first barge-load of immigrants came to be examined. There had been no collision at the Narrows. The ships were safely in, each with its moment of crossing the line recorded to the second. And, scattered among them at their piers, were 2,000 men, women and children who were 'excess quota.' Here by our country's permission, the 2,000 would now be turned back, at the very gate, by our country's mandate.*

> *In a week or two they all went back. I was powerless. I could only watch them go. Day by day the barges took them from Ellis Island back to the ships again, back to the ocean, back to what? As they trooped aboard the big barges under my window, carrying their heavy bundles, some in their quaint, colorful native costumes worn to celebrate their first glad day in free America, some carrying little American flags, most of them quietly weeping, they twisted something in my heart that hurts to this day.[5]*

Women traveling unaccompanied were detained until a male relative came to get them.

LEFT AND FAR RIGHT: *A Polish passport, issued to a mother and child who came to America in 1922.*

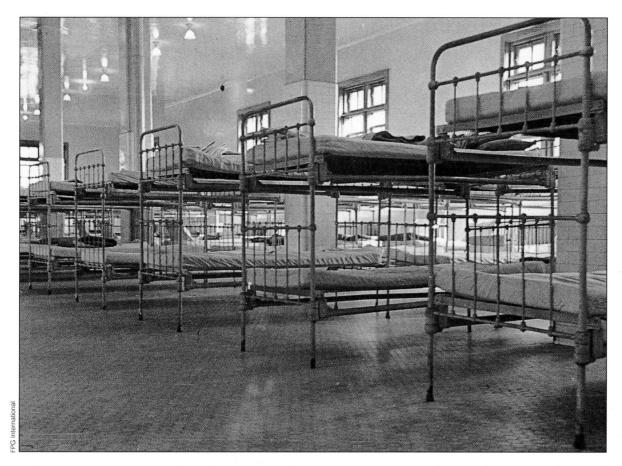

FPG International

Courtesy National Park Service/Ellis Island Collection

The hospital and contagious disease wards contained beds for over 700 patients.

Curran's sympathy for the rejected newcomers was shared by a number of Americans, but the overwhelming sentiment was moving the other way, toward new curbs on immigration.

In May 1924, Congress supplanted the earlier quota act with an even more restrictive measure. It limited annual immigration to 2 percent of a nation's population in the United States as of the 1890 census. This had the effect of giving northern and western Europe 85.6 percent of the total, with just 12.4 percent for immigrants from southern and eastern Europe.

The law also set quotas for the increasing number of immigrants coming from Central America and Canada and finally enacted the change long suggested by commissioners at Ellis Island—it moved the inspection process to

Courtesy National Park Service/Ellis Island Collection

American consulates overseas, requiring immigrants to obtain visas in their countries of origin before setting out for the United States. Under the new law, no more than 10 percent of a country's visas could be issued in any one month, and the visas expired rather quickly. This provision effectively ended the rush of ships to Ellis Island at the beginning of each month and averted the "excess quota" rejections that had so disturbed Curran. The law's other main effect was to greatly reduce the number of people coming through Ellis Island. From the time it opened, until 1924, the island had received 71 percent of all immigrants to the United States. After 1924, until it closed in 1954, Ellis Island received an average of just 56 percent of the nation's immigrants each year.

LEFT: *This photo of a young Polish immigrant came from the identification card issued by the Ellis Island authorities. These cards, listing name, country of origin, and status, were issued to all immigrants.*

In 1928, the commissioner general of immigration commented on the change:

> *Prior to 1924 when the last quota law was enacted, the great bulk of immigration poured through our seaports, and Ellis Island, New York Harbor, as the great portal—the gateway through which the immigrant entered the land of opportunity. The land border ports were of secondary importance. If the expressions 'Ellis Island' and 'immigration' were not synonymous, one could hardly think of the one without thinking of the other. Ellis Island was the great outpost of the new and vigorous Republic. Ellis Island stood guard over the wide-flung portal. Ellis Island resounded for years to the tramp of an endless invading army....Ellis Island is freed of this inundating horde and largely freed of carping critics, but Ellis Island has lost its proud place in the grand immigration scheme.[6]*

FPG International

OPPOSITE: *Two young Irishmen stare out at the New York City skyline.*

On a quiet day in 1926, a small gathering of new arrivals heads for the Main Building. This sparse, orderly group stands in *sharp contrast to the vast hordes of people who crowded under the canopy just a few years earlier.*

By 1983, this skeleton was all that was left of a greenhouse that
stood on Ellis Island when it was a thriving receiving station.

116

DECLINE AND REDISCOVERY OF ELLIS ISLAND

After 1924, immigration through Ellis Island never exceeded 190,000 a year; often the number of immigrants coming through was much lower. During the Great Depression of the 1930s, more people left the United States than entered, many voluntarily and some through deportation. President Herbert Hoover ordered consulates overseas to evaluate immigrants to make sure no one likely "to become a public charge" gained entry to America while so many U.S. citizens were unemployed.

The strictly-enforced immigration laws left Ellis Island without a purpose, and in 1934, President Franklin Roosevelt's secretary of labor, Francis Perkins, appointed

117

a committee to make recommendations for changes and improvements on the island. In its report, the committee described how different the receiving station had become in the years since World War I:

> *Because of the vast number of immigrants previously handled, the buildings on Island No. 1 have always taken on something of the quality of barracks and though possessing proper sanitation and more than adequate light and air, they represent today an outmoded institutional plant unsuited to present day needs.*
>
> *For the 10 years preceding the war almost 1 million aliens a year came to the port of New York. Of these all third-class passengers were regularly sent to Ellis Island. The handling of vast numbers of persons, whose language for the most part we could not speak, was an administrative task of such porportions that it was bound to produce many hardships and misunderstandings, and in consequence the myth of cruelty and bureaucracy grew until the very name 'Ellis Island' was one at which the alien shuddered.*

A party of American religious leaders inspecting the facilities in 1933 posed with a group of immigrant children. By this time, immigration had dwindled to a mere fraction of what it once was.

FPG International

Today, in 1934, quite another set of conditions awaits the arriving alien. In the old days all immigrants went to Ellis Island as a matter of routine and were discharged from there. Now there is a rigid inspection of the alien before embarkation, a second medical examination aboard ship, and an inspection of his immigration papers before landing. Consequently, comparatively few immigrants are held for further examination at Ellis Island.

In the fiscal year ended June 30, 1933, only 4,488 incoming aliens, including both immigrants and visitors, were held at Ellis Island, usually for not more than two or three days…[at the same time] some 7,037 outgoing aliens passed through Ellis Island. The majority of those aliens whom we are returning to the land of their birth, wait here for their passports and sailing arrangements. Sometimes they wait for long periods of time. The foreign consuls are frequently slow in granting passports, as they want to satisfy themselves by careful investigation that these people are nationals whom they should take back.[1]

FPG International

Immigration commissioner Rudolph Reimer gave presents at a Christmas party on Ellis Island in 1934. The little boy in the center was on his way to Milwaukee from Germany, but the other children were not so lucky—their parents were being deported.

The report went on to make recommendations for procedural changes at Ellis Island, and it called for major repair work on the buildings. In response, $1.1 million was authorized, and over the next two years a new building was erected to house arriving immigrants so they would not have to mix with deportees. But the number of newcomers detained was so small and the costs of operating the building so great that it fell into disuse.

By 1940, with world tensions mounting, Congress became worried that some immigrants from Europe might pose a threat to national security. As a result, the Immigration and Naturalization Service was transferred from the Department of Labor to the Department of Justice, and the attorney general became the official responsible for Ellis Island.

During World War II, the island was used almost exclusively as a detention center for enemy aliens—Germans, Italians, Japanese, Hungarians, Romanians, and Bulgarians—and many spent up to six months there awaiting resolution of their status. *The New York Times* visited the center in 1942 and reported a typical day among those held:

> *Their guards march them to breakfast in the big dining room at 7:30, Germans and Italians together, Japs separately. Dinner is at 12, outdoor exercise begins at 3 if they want it, supper at 5:15 and taps at 10. It leaves a good deal of time to be got through somehow, and the immigration officials do their best to keep the time from hanging too heavily.*

> *Their guests are allowed all the newspapers and magazines they want. They draw on the island library as often as they like. The American Tract Society has stocked it with some 20,000 volumes in about 30 languages. Subject to censorship, they write and receive letters. They telephone under strict supervision. They receive visits from wives, business partners, lawyers, and others whom they have legitimate reasons for seeing.[2]*

Courtesy National Park Service/Ellis Island Collection

NOTICE

Breakfast	from 7.30 a. m.
Dinner	" 12.— noon
Supper	" 5.— p. m.

SITTING

After the war, activity on Ellis Island waned once again, and there were calls to close it. It had one more flurry of activity, during the Cold War in 1950. The new Internal Security Act required deportation of any member of a communist or fascist organization, no matter how peripheral the affiliation. People detained under this law generally went through Ellis Island. There was an outcry at some of the injustices perpetrated in the name of national security, and the law was eased in 1951, allowing deportation only of active members of the feared political organizations.

OPPOSITE: *By 1951, the once-packed Registry Room was quiet, its vast spaces empty save for a few immigrant families waiting to be processed.*

Over the next several years, an increasing number of people complained that Ellis Island had outlived its usefulness as an immigration station. They eventually prevailed; Ellis Island was formally closed on November 12, 1954. *The New York Times* reported the event:

> *Without ceremony, the career of Ellis Island as an immigration station came to a virtual close yesterday.*
>
> *The last detained alien—a Norwegian seaman who had overstayed his shore leave—was a passenger on the Battery-bound ferry at 10:15 a.m....The peak of immigrant traffic through Ellis Island came in 1907 when 1,200,000 persons were examined there. But gradually, as admission and detention procedures changed, the alien population decreased.*
>
> *As [Attorney General Herbert] Brownell explained Thursday, "The little island between the Statue of Liberty and the skyline and piers of New York seems to have served its purpose for immigration."[3]*

In the years that followed, many proposals were made for selling or redeveloping Ellis Island, but nothing came of them. The buildings remained unused, vulnerable to vandals and the ravages of the elements. In 1965, President Lyndon Johnson declared

Most of the buildings on Ellis Island have fallen into a state of decay, as the crumbling plaster of this hospital ward shows. The Statue of Liberty/Ellis Island Foundation hopes eventually to restore all the historical structures.

© Susan Livingston

Guastavens
ceeling —

Flles Island
Closed on Nov 12
1954

Gustavino
ceeling.

© Klaus Schnitzer

the island a national monument, and made it part of the Statue of Liberty National Monument, to be administered by the National Park Service under the Department of the Interior.

It was not until the 1980s, however, with the approaching centennials of both the Statue of Liberty in 1986 and Ellis Island in 1992, that definite plans were put into motion for restoring the Ellis Island buildings and creating a museum of immigration.

Among the rubble in the painter's shop were remnants of one of the original pigments used in mixing paint.

The Department of the Interior chose a private group, The Statue of Liberty/Ellis Island Foundation, to raise funds from the public for the design and construction of a museum. Since the plans were announced, more than twenty million Americans have contributed to the $160 million project.

The Foundation had hoped to restore all five structures on the northern end of the site, but the budget permitted only the restoring of the Main Building, refitting of the Powerhouse, and stabilizing of the Kitchen and Laundry Building with weatherproof-

ing and a new roof.

Two architectural firms, both well known for their sensitive and meticulous restoration and renovation work, were chosen for the project. Beyer Blinder Belle of New York and Notter Finegold + Alexander of Boston and

Washington, DC, formed an association to work on the Ellis Island restoration, the largest renovation project ever undertaken in the United States. Their mandate was to preserve the Ellis Island Main Building as a landmark while also converting it to a museum that would commemorate the immigrant experience.

Before beginning any work, the design teams embarked on a significant research project, analyzing the buildings architecturally and historically, pinpointing all changes and alterations made over the years, and documenting the uses of each room over time. The result was a massive 12-volume report, in which the most important areas, both architecturally and historically, were "graded". Areas with the most significance would be restored faithfully, while less important spaces would be adapted for modern museum needs.

The Baggage and Dormitory Building, which once housed the dining area shown below, and opposite below, has fallen into disrepair, with a rotted roof and weeds growing through the floor.

The design team decided to restore the Main Building to its 1918 to 1924 period. During that time it reached architectural maturity with the installation in the Great Hall of the vaulted white-tiled Guastavino ceiling in 1918 and saw 1,662,613 immigrants pass through.

Ellis Island had lain abandoned for nearly thirty years when the project began. The effects of this neglect were devastating—salt water had seeped through the masonry in the Main Building; portions of roofing had rotted through, letting in rain and snow; debris filled some rooms waist high; floors were rotted; and trees and weeds grew among the debris.

Before any physical work could be done, the building had to be stabilized and dried out. To prevent warping and buckling, the moisture had to be drawn out slowly—the solution was to place two large heaters outside the building and use pressurized dry air

125

inside the building. The drying out process took two years. Roof tiles were repaired and replaced, and the Main Building was entirely reroofed. The facade was cleaned with low pressure steam, bricks were repointed, and the windows repaired—leaving the original sashes.

© Christopher Barnes

Tulips bloom in front of the partially restored Main Building with its new canopy.

OPPOSITE: *This view of the Great Hall midway through the restoration shows both levels and gives a sense of the massive size of the Main Building.*

The Main Building's four 14-foot (4-m) wide domes had deteriorated so drastically that several years before the current renovation, concrete parging had been poured over them to prevent further weakening. BBB/NFA removed the protective coverings and repaired the brickwork and wooden lattices that supported the domes' copper skins. The original copper had been stripped from the domes by vandals, so new copper sheathings replaced them. These will turn the same brilliant blue-green that once made the domes landmarks. New copper finials were created and flown into place by helicopter.

In the original design of the Main Building, a cast iron and glass canopy covering a paved promenade had connected the building to the water. Although replication would have been possible using historic photographs and drawings, National Park Service restoration guidelines discourage such replicas. Instead, the design team created a

new canopy in steel and glass that evokes the original in spirit and design. Like all new metalwork in the project, it has been painted "Ellis Island Red."

During the clean up, layers of peeling paint revealed traces of graffiti left by immigrants on the original walls. In the detention and waiting rooms, restorers noted initials and dates, poems, cartoons, flowers, religious symbols, and comments written on the plaster in pencil and in the blue chalk used by inspectors. These have been restored, and will be on view.

Once inside, visitors to Ellis Island will be able to follow the paths of the immigrants. Entering the Main Building under the canopy, they will come into the Baggage Room, where new arrivals once checked their bags before proceeding to inspections. The Baggage Room has been modernized and is to be used for orientation of visitors and exhibit space.

Immigrants next climbed the Registry Room stairs, undergoing the "sixty-second medical" examination as they ascended. This staircase had been removed at an earlier date, and no record remained of the original plans. Since the walk up the stairs was critical to the immigrants' experiences, however, it was essential that it be recreated. Using compatible contemporary materials (so as not to confuse a historic artifact with the modern recreation), the architects rebuilt the stairway, so that visitors will be able to relive the stair climb.

Once in the Registry Room, immigrants underwent a legal inspection. This room, the centerpiece of the project, has been restored to its 1920 appearance. Rafael Guastavino, a Spaniard who came to America with his son in 1881, installed the vaulted, tiled ceiling in 1918. The vaults are constructed of three layers of thin terra

OPPOSITE: *A painter at work in the east wing of the Main Building.*

The Great Hall (Registry Room) during restoration. Note the sparkling whiteness of the tiles in the Guastavino ceiling compared to its pre-restoration condition in the photograph on page 123.

© Klaus Schnitzer

cotta tiles set in beds of concrete. During the restoration, each of the 28,282 tiles was checked—to Guastavino's credit, only 17 needed replacement or repair.

The mezzanine level walls of the Registry Room were finished with Caen stone, a plaster that mimics limestone, which was popular at the turn of the century. The architects conducted extensive research and experiments, which eventually enabled them to successfully recreate the long-lost formula.

Museum visitors will also experience "The Stair of Separation," which will take them down to the Railroad Ticket Office. Here the exhibit "The Peopling of America" describes where the immigrants who passed through Ellis Island settled in their new country.

The Special Inquiry rooms, where immigrants pled their cases from behind wooden railings, contain exhibits relating to the inspections. A fragment of the original railing was used to recreate the railings now in place.

A Dormitory Room, where a detainee might spend days or weeks, has been restored to its 1908 state with triple-tiered bunks. The east wing, where roof gardens were once used for exercise and fresh air, then were converted to offices and dormitories in 1914, now houses the exhibit titled "Treasures From Home," which showcases items the immigrants brought to America.

Original fixtures were used whenever possible during the refitting of the rooms, including 37 sinks, 190 radiators, and 51 toilets.

In addition to the exhibits, museum features include a library and reading room, an oral history center with recording equipment, two 146-seat movie theaters, a curatorial complex, a restaurant, a museum shop, and meeting rooms. Future plans call for a center for genealogical study.

Visitors can reach Ellis Island via three ferries, departing from Battery Park at the tip of Manhattan, from Liberty State Park in Jersey City, New Jersey, and from the Statue of Liberty.

OPPOSITE: *The post-reconstruction Registry Room, shown here before the installation of museum exhibitry.*

National Park Service/photo: Brian Feeney

The Special Inquiry Rooms are devoted to exhibits that will help visitors to understand the inspection process.

Chronology of the Restoration

1965

President Johnson designates Ellis Island a part of the Statue of Liberty National Monument

1976

Ellis Island opens to the public for limited National Park Services tours

1979–1982

General management plan developed by National Park Service

1982

Statue of Liberty/Ellis Island Foundation formed. Beyer Blinder Belle/Notter Finegold + Alexander, Inc. retained as architects

1983

Restoration begins. "Historic Structures Report" prepared and master plan and interpretive design developed

1984

Drying out of Main Building and debris removal

1985

Construction mobilization, terra cotta tile testing, graffiti identification and conservation, commencing of roofing work and masonry cleaning

1986

Window replacement begins, major demolition commences, construction of temporary bridge to New Jersey for use by construction vehicles, steam cleaning of Main Building, boilers placed in Powerhouse, Guastavino tiles cleaned and repaired

1987

Installation of new structural steel, ornamental copper applied to domes, erection of new Powerhouse chimney, cleaning and restoration of all interior marble and stone, copper finials lowered by helicopter, foundations poured for new canopy

1988

Erection of new canopy steel framework, Caen stone repair and replacement, Registry Room staircase rebuilt, raised chandeliers in Registry Room, commenced stabilization of Kitchen and Laundry Building roof

1989

Painting, plastering, ceramic installation, new oak floors, installation of mechanical, electrical, and plumbing systems, steel frame in place for canopy

1990

Construction finished, exhibitry installed, restoration complete. Grand opening to visitors

ABOVE LEFT: *The new steel-and-glass canopy protects the promenade into the Main Building.*

LEFT: *The Great Hall of the Main Building (where the Registry Room was located) shown here during the reconstruction.*

The architects set aside the portions of the buildings deemed less historically significant for functions such as administration, cataloging, and curatorial uses.

National Park Service/photo: Brian Feeney

133

A P P E N D I X   I

UNITED STATES IMMIGRATION
1892–1954

Year	Through Port of New York	Total U.S.	Year	Through Port of New York	Total U.S.
1892	445,987	579,663	1908	585,970	782,870
1893	343,422	439,730	1909	580,617	751,786
1894	219,046	285,631	1910	786,094	1,041,570
1895	190,928	258,536	1911	637,003	878,587
1896	263,709	343,267	1912	605,151	838,172
1897	180,556	230,832	1913	892,653	1,197,892
1898	178,748	229,299	1914	878,052	1,218,480
1899	242,573	311,715	1915	178,416	326,700
1900	341,712	448,572	1916	141,390	298,826
1901	388,931	487,918	1917	129,446	295,403
1902	493,262	648,743	1918	28,867	110,618
1903	631,835	857,046	1919	26,731	141,132
1904	606,019	812,870	1920	225,206	430,001
1905	788,219	1,026,499	1921	560,971	805,228
1906	880,036	1,100,735	1922	209,778	309,556
1907	1,004,756	1,285,349	1923	295,473	522,919
			1924	315,587	706,896

Total: **14,277,144**   **20,003,041**

(71 percent of total)

Year	Through Port of New York	Total U.S.	Year	Through Port of New York	Total U.S.
1925	137,492	294,314	1940	48,408	70,756
1926	149,289	304,488	1941	23,622	51,776
1927	165,510	335,175	1942	10,173	28,781
1928	157,887	307,255	1943	1,089	23,725
1929	158,238	279,678	1944	1,075	28,551
1930	147,982	241,700	1945	2,636	38,119
1931	63,392	97,139	1946	52,050	108,721
1932	21,500	35,576	1947	83,884	147,292
1933	12,944	23,068	1948	104,665	170,570
1934	17,574	29,470	1949	113,050	188,317
1935	23,173	34,956	1950	166,849	249,187
1936	23,434	36,329	1951	142,903	205,717
1937	31,644	50,244	1952	183,222	265,520
1938	44,846	67,395	1953	87,483	170,434
1939	62,035	82,998	1954	98,813	208,177

Total: 2,336,862 4,175,428

(56 percent of total)

Statistics from Historic Resource Study, Statue of Liberty/Ellis Island, by Harlan D. Unrah, U.S. Department of the Interior/National Park Service.

APPENDIX II

TRACING YOUR ANCESTRY THROUGH ELLIS ISLAND

The fascinating stories of the immigrant experience inspire many people to delve into their own family histories. A number of resources are available to those who wish to trace their ancestry through Ellis Island.

Before you begin, it is important to have collected certain necessary pieces of information. These include:

- the names of your parents, grandparents, and great-grandparents, and if possible, names of any ancestors from earlier generations.
- vital statistics—the dates of events in your ancestors' lives, including birth, marriage, and death.
- the places of origin—where your ancestors lived, and the dates they lived there.

Once you have this information, your genealogical research will have already begun.

The following agencies hold important records for your search:

**United States Department of Justice
Immigration and Naturalization Service
Records Verification Center
1446-21 Edwin Miller Boulevard
Martinsburg, WV 25401**

Provides arrival records at the port of New York since June 16, 1897; records from other Eastern seaboard ports since 1891; and naturalization records after September 27, 1906. Request form G-641 (Application for Verification of Information from Immigration and Naturalization Service Records).

**The New England Historic Genealogical Society
101 Newbury Street
Boston, MA 02116**

Maintains a complete set of Massachusetts vital records from 1841 to 1895, local histories of all states and Canadian provinces, and a 15,000-volume collection on European families. Considered an excellent resource for information about Irish and British families.

**The National Archives and Records Service
Reference Services Branch
Washington, DC 20408**

Provides manifests (immigration passenger lists) on microfilm, dating from 1883 to 1845. A pamphlet, "Using Records in the National Archives for Genealogical Research," is also available.

**The Federal Archives And Records Center
Archives Branch, GSA Building 22
The Military Ocean Terminal
Bayonne, NJ 07002-5388
(201) 923-7252**

Provides manifests for passengers who arrived at New York from 1820 to 1897, plus an index for the manifests from 1820 to 1946.

**The Genealogical Society Library
The Church of Jesus Christ of the Latter Day Saints
50 North Temple Street
Salt Lake City, Utah 84105**

Provides a computerized index of 60 million immigrants, both members of the Church and non-members.

The following bibliography, provided by the library at the Statue of Liberty National Monument, is an excellent source of genealogical information.

Baxter, Angus. *In Search of Your British And Irish Roots.* Genealogical Publishing Company. Baltimore, 1982.

Baxter, Angus. *In Search of Your Canadian Roots.* Genealogical Publishing Company. Baltimore, 1989.

Baxter, Angus. *In Search of Your European Roots.* Genealogical Publishing Company. Baltimore, 1985.

Camp, Anthony. *Everyone Has Roots—An Introduction to English Genealogy.* W.H. Allen & Company, Limited. London, 1978; Genealogical Publishing Company. Baltimore, 1978.

Coleman, Terry. *Going To America.* Genealogical Publishing Company. Baltimore, 1972.

Durrie, Daniel S. (ed.). *Index to American Genealogies.* Originally published by John Munsell's Sons, Albany, New York, in 1900. Genealogical Publishing Company. Baltimore, 1967.

Eakle, Arlene & Johni Cerny. *The Source: A Guide Book of American Genealogy.* Ancestry Publishing Company. Salt Lake City, 1984.

Ellis, Eilish. *Emigrants From Ireland, 1847–52, State Aided Emigration Schemes from Crown Estates in Ireland.* Genealogical Publishing Company. Baltimore, 1978.

Esker, Katie-Prince, ed. *The Genealogical Department—Source Records from the Daughters of the American Revolution Magazine, 1947–1950.* Genealogical Publishing Company. Baltimore, 1975.

Glazier, Ira & Michael Tepper, eds. *The Famine Immigrants—List of Irish Immigrants Arriving at the Port of New York 1846–1851.* Genealogical Publishing Company. Baltimore, 1985.

Greenwood, Val. *The Researcher's Guide to American Genealogy.* Genealogical Publishing Company. Baltimore, 1988.

Hackett, J.D. & Chas. Montague Early. *Passenger Lists From Ireland.* Genealogical Publishing Company. Baltimore, 1981.

Hamilton-Edwards, Gerald. *In Search of Scottish Ancestry.* Genealogical Publishing Company. Baltimore, 1986.

Jacobus, Donald. *Index To Genealogical Periodicals.* Genealogical Publishing Company. Baltimore, 1932.

Kaminkov, Jack & Marion (transcribers). *A List of Emigrants from England to America, 1718–1759.* Genealogical Publishing Company. Baltimore, 1984.

Kaminkov, Marion. *Genealogies in the Library of Congress.* The Magna Carta Book Company. Baltimore, 1987.

Knittle, Walter. *Early Eighteenth Century Palatine Emigration.* Genealogical Publishing Company. Baltimore, 1937.

Markwell, F.C. & Pauline Saul. *The A–Z Guide to Tracing Ancestors in Britain*. Genealogical Publishing Company. Baltimore, 1985.

Mitchell, Brian. *Irish Emigration Lists, 1833–39*. (Londonderry & Antrim counties). Genealogical Publishing Company. Baltimore, 1989.

Mitchell, Brian. *Irish Passenger List, 1847–71*. Genealogical Publishing Company. Baltimore, 1988.

O'Brian, Michael J. *A Hidden Phase of American History—Ireland's Part in America's Struggle for Liberty*. Genealogical Publishing Company. Baltimore, 1919.

O'Callaghan, Edmund Bailey. *List of Inhabitants of Colonial New York*. Genealogical Publishing Company. Baltimore, 1979.

Pine, L.G. *American Origins*. Genealogical Publishing Company. Baltimore, 1980.

Rasmussen, Louis. *San Francisco Ship Passenger Lists*. Genealogical Publishing Company. Baltimore, 1978.

Tepper, Michael. *American Passenger Arrival Records*. Genealogical Publishing Company. Baltimore, 1988.

U.S. Census Bureau. *A Century of Population Growth—1790–1900*. Genealogical Publishing Company. Baltimore, originally published in 1909.

Yoder, Donald, ed. *Rhineland Emigrants*. Genealogical Publishing Company. Baltimore, 1985.

Zimmerman, Gary & Marion Wolfert. *German Immigrants—Lists of Passengers Bound from Bremerhaven to New York: 1847–1867*. Three vols. Genealogical Publishing Company. Baltimore, 1985.

Morton Allen Directory of European Passenger Steamship Arrivals. Genealogical Publishing Company. Baltimore, 1931.

New World Immigrants: Ship Passenger Lists from Periodicals. Genealogical Publishing Company. Baltimore, 1979.

Passenger Arrivals at the Port of Baltimore, 1820–34 (U.S. Customs Records). Genealogical Publishing Company. Baltimore, 1982.

Passengers to America—A Consolidation of Ship Passenger Lists from the New England Historical & Genealogical Register. Genealogical Publishing Company. Baltimore, 1988.

ENDNOTES

Chapter 1. Castle Garden

1. Charles Dickens, *American Notes* (New York: International Publishing Corp., 1985), 221-223.
2. Kerby A. Miller, *Emigrants and Exiles* (New York: Oxford University Press Inc., 1985), 292.
3. Ibid., 263.
4. Ibid., 263.
5. *Harper's New Monthly Magazine,* March 1871.
6. Robert Louis Stevenson, *The Amateur Emigrant* (New York: Charles Scribner's Sons, 1905), 83-84.
7. "Castle Garden's Monopoly: Cogent Reasons for the Abolition of the Emigration Commission," *The World,* 27 July 1887, 5.
8. "What the Clergyman Said: Advising Scandinavian Immigrants to Avoid Castle Garden," *The World,* 25 Aug. 1887, 1.

Chapter 2. The Golden Doorway into America Opens

1. Thomas M. Pitkin, *Keepers of the Gate: A History of Ellis Island* (New York: New York University Press, 1975).
2. "Mr. Windom Explains: No Other Site, He Says, for an Immigrant Station," *The World,* 7 March 1890, 5.
3. "Landed on Ellis Island," *The New York Times,* 2 Jan. 1892, 1.

Chapter 3. The Great Hall Fire and The Era of Reform

1. "Fire on Ellis Island: Many Buildings Burn," *New York Tribune,* 15 June 1897, 1.
2. "New Immigration Station: Will Be Ready for Use by Dec. 15," *The New York Times,* 3 Dec. 1900, 5.
3. Terence V. Powderly, *The Path I Trod: The Autobiography of Terence V. Powderly* (New York: Columbia University Press, 1940).
4. Edward Steiner, *On the Trail of the Immigrant* (New York: Fleming H. Revell Co., 1906), 139.
5. Pitkin, *History of Ellis Island.*
6. Harlan D. Unrah, *Statue of Liberty/Ellis Island Historic Resource Study* (Washington: U.S. Department of the Interior/National Park Service, 1984).
7. Mary J. Shapiro, *Gateway to Liberty: The Story of the Statue of Liberty and Ellis Island* (New York: Vintage Books, 1986), 149.
8. "President Starts Ellis Island Inquiry: Astonishes Officials by Naming Special Commission," *The New York Times,* 17 Sept. 1903, 1.
9. Unrah, *Statue of Liberty/Ellis Island.*

Chapter 4. Island of Hope, Island of Tears

1. Edward Corsi, *In the Shadow of Liberty: The Chronicle of Ellis Island* (New York: The Macmillan Co., 1935), 3–4.
2. David M. Brownstone, Irene M. Franck, and Douglass L. Brownstone, *Island of Hope, Island of Tears* (New York: Rawson, Wade Publishers, 1979), 144.

3. Unrah, *Statue of Liberty/Ellis Island*, 2: 551–552.

4. Irving Howe and Kenneth Libo, *How We Lived* (New York: St. Martin's Press/Marke, 1979), 21.

5. Brownstone et al., *Island of Hope*.

6. Fiorello LaGuardia, *The Making of an Insurgent: An Autobiography, 1882–1919* (New York: Capricorn Books, 1961), 64.

7. Unrah, *Statue of Liberty/Ellis Island*, 111.

8. LaGuardia, *Autobiography*, 65–66.

9. Unrah, *Statue of Liberty/Ellis Island*, 11–14.

10. Cecyle S. Neidle, *The New Americans* (New York: Twayne Publishers, 1967), 293.

11. Corsi, *Chronicle of Ellis Island*.

12. Louis Adamic, *Laughing in the Jungle: The Autobiography of an Immigrant in America* (New York: Harper, 1932), 40–45.

Chapter 5. The Old Country

1. Miller, *Emigrants and Exiles*, 281.

2. Ibid., 283.

3. Ibid., 285.

4. Lewis Namier, *1848: The Revolution of the Intellectuals* (Garden City: Anchor Books, Doubleday & Co. Inc., 1964), 3.

5. Theodore Blegen, *Land of Their Choice: The Immigrants Write Home* (Minneapolis: University of Minnesota Press, 1955).

6. Namier, *Revolution*, 3.

7. Mary Antin, *The Promised Land* (New York: Houghton Mifflin Co., 1940).

Chapter 6. Deportation Delirium

1. Frederic C. Howe, *The Confessions of a Reformer* (New York: Charles Scribner's Sons, 1925), 273–274.

2. Ibid., 327.

3. Pitkin, *History of Ellis Island*, 124.

4. Unrah, *Statue of Liberty/Ellis Island*, 816.

5. "Prisoners Taken in Raids: Hurried to This Port for Deportation," *The New York Times*, 4 Jan. 1920, 1.

Chapter 7. Revival and Restriction

1. Brownstone et al., *Island of Hope*, 227.

2. Pitkin, *History of Ellis Island*, 137.

3. Shapiro, *Gateway to Liberty*, 137.

4. Henry H. Curran, *Pillar to Post* (New York: Charles Scribner's Sons, 1941), 87.

5. Ibid., 87.

6. Unrah, *Statue of Liberty/Ellis Island*, 127.

Chapter 8. Decline and Rediscovery of Ellis Island

1. Unrah, *Statue of Liberty/Ellis Island*, 1,012.

2. Clair Price, "Harbor Camp for Enemy Aliens," *New York Times Magazine*, 25 Jan. 1942, 29.

3. "Ellis Island Ends Alien Processing," *The New York Times*, 13 Nov. 1954, 20.

INDEX